USAF WARRIOR STUDIES

Richard H. Kohn and Joseph P. Harahan
General Editors

D1616803

USAF Warrior Studies

Air Superiority in World War II and Korea, edited by Richard H. Kohn and
Joseph P. Harahan, 1983
GPO Stock #008-070-0489-5

The Command of the Air, by Giulio Douhet, New Imprint, 1983
GPO Stock #008-070-050-1

*Condensed Analysis of the Ninth Air Force in the European Theater of
Operations*, 1984
GPO Stock #008-070-0513-1

The Literature of Aeronautics, Astronautics, and Air Power, by Richard P.
Hallion, 1984
GPO Stock #008-070-0523-9

Over The Hump, by William H. Tunner, New Imprint, 1985
For distribution within the U.S. Department of Defense only

Air Interdiction in World War II, Korea, and Vietnam, edited by Richard H.
Kohn and Joseph P. Harahan, 1986
GPO Stock #008-070-00571-9

Air Leadership, edited by Wayne Thompson, 1986
GPO Stock #008-070-00580-81

The Strategic Air War Against Germany and Japan: A Memoir, by Haywood
S. Hansell, Jr., 1986
GPO Stock #008-070-00583-2

The Organization and Lineage of the United States Air Force, by Charles
Ravenstein, 1986
GPO Stock #008-070-00570-1

Makers of the United States Air Force, edited by John L. Frisbee, 1987
GPO Stock #008-070-00593-0

General Kenney Reports, by George C. Kenney, New Imprint, 1987
For distribution within the U.S. Department of Defense only

ULTRA and the Army Air Forces in World War II, edited by Diane T.
Putney, 1987
GPO Stock #008-070-00600-6

Strategic Air Warfare

An Interview with Generals Curtis E. LeMay,
Leon W. Johnson, David A. Burchinal,
and Jack J. Catton

Edited with an Introduction by
Richard H. Kohn and Joseph P. Harahan

Office of Air Force History
United States Air Force
Washington, D.C., 1988

Library of Congress Cataloging-in-Publication Data

Strategic air warfare.

   (USAF warrior studies)
   Bibliography: p.
   Includes index.
   Supt. of Docs. no.: D 301.96:st8/2
      1. Bombing, Aerial—United States. 2. World War, 1939–1945—Aerial oper-
ations, American. 3. Korean War, 1950–1953—Aerial operations, American. 4.
Vietnamese Conflict, 1961–1975—Aerial operations, American. 5. United States.
Air Force—History. 6. Generals—United States—Interviews. I. Le May, Curtis E.
II. Kohn, Richard H. III. Harahan, Joseph P. IV. United States. Air Force.
Office of Air Force History. V. Series
UG703.277 1988   358.4'2'0973   88–600389
ISBN 0–912799–56–0

Project Warrior Studies are published by the Office of Air Force History.
The views expressed in this publication are those of the contributors and do
not necessarily reflect the policies of the United States Air Force or the
Department of Defense.

For sale by the Superintendent of Documents, U.S. Government Printing Office
Washington, D.C. 20402

Foreword

Strategic Air Warfare is part of a continuing series of historical volumes produced by the Office of Air Force History in direct support of Project Warrior. Since its beginnings, in 1982, Project Warrior has captured the imagination of Air Force people around the world and reawakened a keener appreciation of our fundamental purpose as a Service: to deter war, but to be prepared to fight and win should deterrence fail.

Military history helps provide a realistic perspective on warfare. Through the study of past events, we gain insight into the capabilities of armed forces and, most importantly, a sound knowledge of the policies, strategies, tactics, doctrine, leadership, and weapons that have produced success in battle. Each of us, in broadening our knowledge of air power's past, helps to maintain the most effective Air Force possible, now and in the future.

LARRY D. WELCH, General, USAF
Chief of Staff

United States Air Force
Historical Advisory Committee
(As of August 1, 1988)

Alfred D. Chandler
Harvard University

Charles R. Hamm
Lieutenant General, USAF
Superintendent, USAF Academy

Anne Foreman
The General Counsel, USAF

Ralph E. Havens
Lieutenant General, USAF
Commander, Air University

Norman A. Graebner
The University of Virginia

John H. Morrow, Jr.
The University of Tennessee at Knoxville
(*Chairman*)

Dominick Graham
Royal Military College of Canada

Thomas M. Ryan, Jr.
General, USAF (Retired)

Ira D. Gruber
Rice University

Gerhard L. Weinberg
University of North Carolina at
    Chapel Hill

Contents

Illustrations

Introduction

Early in June 1984 some thirty-five of the retired four-star generals of the United States Air Force gathered in Washington, D.C., for the annual Senior Statesmen Conference. Each year since the early 1960s the Air Force has invited its retired four-star generals to Washington. From that group in 1984, the Office of Air Force History invited four general officers—Generals Curtis E. LeMay, Leon W. Johnson, David A. Burchinal, and Jack J. Catton—to participate in a group oral interview on the history of strategic air warfare. They accepted and on June 15, 1984, at Bolling Air Force Base, the four discussed for nearly three hours the development and evolution of strategic air warfare. Because the session ended without time for a discussion of the Cuban Missile Crisis and the Vietnam War, the four conferred again, this time by telephone, to discuss these and other issues not considered earlier. This interview was the third in a series begun by the Office of Air Force History with the "senior statesmen," the first in 1982 covering air superiority in World War II and Korea, the second in 1983 discussing the type of aerial interdiction used in World War II, Korea, and Vietnam.

The purpose of the interview was to have the air commanders meet in an informal setting and discuss the development of strategic air employment as a form of warfare. The hope was that in the course of the discussion these men, who had served together for many years and undergone common experiences, might stimulate each other to remember facts and events that have otherwise gone unrecorded, and to flesh out the record with fuller explanations of motives and the reasoning behind great occurrences. The result was beyond our expectations, for almost immediately the four generals began interviewing each other, reminiscing at times, exchanging ideas, questioning circumstances, and recalling motives and objectives clear at the time of decision but clouded over by the passage of time. Often a single question led to four or five others generated from within the group. At one point when they were discussing atomic warfare and the creation of the Strategic Air Command, General LeMay leaned forward and said quietly to General Johnson, "Let me tell you what I was trying to do. . . ."

1

STRATEGIC AIR WARFARE

The Strategic Air Command was but one of many issues discussed. Beginning with preparations for World War II and the concepts underlying planning, training, and equipping American air forces for the strategic bombing of Germany and Japan, the participants explained their roles: in the war in flying and commanding bombing missions and campaigns; in creating the atomic air forces in the immediate postwar years; in building and molding the Strategic Air Command in the 1950s; in advising and making decisions during the Cuban Missile Crisis; and in leading and observing the Air Force during the limited war in Southeast Asia.

The Office of Air Force History chose strategic air warfare as the topic because it is a distinctive aspect of air warfare that has molded and defined the United States Air Force since the 1920s. From the writings of Billy Mitchell through the great strategic campaigns of World War II to the creation of the nuclear deterrent forces of the 1940s, 1950s, and 1960s, strategic warfare dominated the Air Force, determining the preparations for war, the types of airplanes developed and deployed, and the size and configuration of the service, from the location of its bases to the distinctive decoration on part of its uniforms. The very creation of the Air Force was bound up with the effort to wage independent air war, to use air power against the will and capacity of an enemy nation to wage war in order to decide a conflict without—or independent of—military operations on land or at sea. Thus the Office believed that by exploring the experiences and ideas of some of the senior commanders who led America's strategic air forces in war and peace, it would contribute to an understanding not only of the United States Air Force, but of air power itself. Readers should remember, however, that this interview is not history but the collective memory of four leading airmen; it is the source material upon which history rests. The interview was conducted in person, with the followup discussion completed by telephone two months later. The transcript was edited and partially rearranged to follow a chronological format. Each discussant read and approved the edited transcript, occasionally adding some small fragment of material or editing the text further. The introduction, footnotes, and bibliography were contributed by the editors.

The creation of this interview and its transformation from the spoken word to a finished publication was a group effort by the Air Force History Program. Lt. Col. Maurice Maryanow, Dr. James C. Hasdorff, and Mr. Hugh N. Ahmann of the USAF Historical Research Center contributed questions and did background research prior to the interview. Located in the Center are oral histories of Generals LeMay, Johnson, Burchinal, and Catton. Each were studied before the interview. Mr. John T. Bohn and Mr. J. C. Hopkins of the Strategic Air Command History Office suggested questions and read the final manuscript prior to publication. In the Office of Air Force

History, Col. John F. Shiner, Mr. Herman Wolk, Dr. Alfred M. Beck, and Dr. Walton S. Moody proposed questions, read and critiqued the edited manuscript, and offered suggestions. Sergeant Glenn B. Reynolds typed the manuscript. Mr. Ray Del Villar of the Air Force Publishing Division designed the graphics. Mrs. Laura H. Dahljelm accomplished the copy editing, photograph selection, and final layout before printing. All photographs appearing throughout the volume, unless otherwise noted, are from the U.S. Air Force collection, the Department of Defense Still Media Records, and the National Air and Space Museum. The editors wish also to thank Professors David Rosenberg of the Naval War College and Marc Trachtenberg of the University of Pennsylvania for reading the transcript and offering their judgment that the interview if published would be useful to military historians. To all these individuals, the editors express sincerest thanks.

General Curtis LeMay's early life and education reveal the self-discipline, military inclination, and love of flying that characterized his Air Force career. A midwesterner born in Columbus, Ohio, in November 1906, he considered competing for an appointment to West Point, but lacking personal or family acquaintances with Ohio Congressmen he enrolled instead at Ohio State University. His studies and work preoccupied him: taking civil engineering courses, becoming an honor graduate of the Reserve Officers' Training Corps (ROTC), and working nine hours a night, six days a week, at a local foundry. Appointed a second lieutenant in the U.S. Army Reserves in June 1928, LeMay spent the summer in basic training at Camp Knox, Kentucky, with the 62d Field Artillery Brigade, Field Artillery Reserve. In July he resigned his commission and accepted an officer's commission in the Ohio National Guard. His purpose was to get a priority placement into the Army Air Corps, a feat he achieved in the fall of 1928. After resigning his commission again, he enlisted as a flying cadet and completed basic and advanced pilot training at March Field, California, and Kelly Field, Texas, in 1928–29. Commissioned as a second lieutenant in October 1929, he spent the next decade as a pilot and navigator, serving in fighter and bomber squadrons based in Michigan, Ohio, Hawaii, and Virginia. In January 1937 he had the good fortune to be assigned to Langley Field, Virginia, with the 2d Bombardment Group, the first Army Air Corps unit equipped with new, long-range B–17 bombers. Led by Lt. Col. Robert Olds, who became LeMay's mentor, this group flew B–17s for almost four and a half years before America entered World War II. As an engineer, LeMay studied the

Lt. Curtis E. LeMay.

bomber's characteristics and component systems; later during the war, when he led B–17 bomb groups into combat, this knowledge became the foundation on which he built effective combat forces.

Early in the war, LeMay was assigned to the Eighth Air Force. Given command of the 305th Bombardment Group (35 B–17s) at Muroc Field, California, in April 1942, he trained this inexperienced group briefly, then led it in September to England. Except for LeMay, no one in the group had ever flown or navigated an aircraft across an ocean before. Within days of their arrival they were flying bombing missions over France. Colonel LeMay's 305th Bomb Group was one of VIII Bomber Command's first four combat groups; it remained active in combat throughout the war, flying in virtually every major bombing campaign. LeMay himself flew with the bomb group, was highly decorated, and achieved a reputation for his leadership in combat, his innovations in training, and his development of new bombing techniques. A taciturn, studious bomber commander, LeMay was promoted to brigadier general in September 1943, one year after his arrival in the European theater. Seven months later, in March 1944, he was promoted again to the rank of major general. With rank came larger commands. Remaining within Eighth Air Force, he commanded a wing (146 B–17s) and an air division (3 wings, totaling 266 B–17s and B–24s). He flew with his bomber forces, participating in some of the fiercest air battles of the war, including the Schweinfurt-

Regensburg raids, Big Week, and the early efforts over Normandy and Northern France.

In late June 1944 he left Europe for the Pacific, becoming Commander of the XX Bomber Command, the Army Air Forces' first operational strategic air command in the Pacific. Flying from operational bases in China, the B–29s under his command struck directly at strategic targets in Japan. As the Pacific war intensified in the winter of 1944–45, Gen. Henry H. Arnold, Commanding General, Army Air Forces, decided to concentrate all of the Pacific Theater strategic bombing operations from bases in the Mariana Islands. He ordered LeMay to move his bomber command from China to the Marianas. There, Arnold made LeMay commander of the XXI Bomber Command, a newer and larger command of B–29 bombers. From his new headquarters on Guam, LeMay planned and conducted B–29 strikes against Japanese industries, cities, and military installations. These air strikes devastated Japan and exerted pressure, especially in conjunction with Allied naval operations, on Japanese political and military leaders to surrender. In the war's final months LeMay gained a degree of notoriety, appearing in articles in the *New York Times*, *Colliers*, and *New Yorker*, as well as on the cover of *Time* the week of August 13, 1945, the same week as the atomic bomb attacks on Hiroshima and Nagasaki, Japan.

Public recognition was a consequence of the strategic air war and LeMay's combat record. During World War II LeMay came to be recognized as one of the Army Air Forces' quintessential bomber commanders and operators. His name became synonymous with leading large, powerful strategic air forces. He had trained and led bomber groups; he had developed bomber tactics that improved discipline in the air against attacking fighters and enabled bomb crews to strike targets more accurately; he had led massed formations of bomber wings and divisions on long-range air strikes over Germany; and finally in the Pacific, he had constructed a large, long-range strategic air force, developed new techniques of low-level, incendiary bombing, and conducted a devastating air campaign against the very fabric of the Japanese economy and society.

When the war ended in September 1945, Major General LeMay was but one of the many air leaders who remained in the service to create and build the postwar United States Air Force. At thirty-eight, however, he was one of the service's youngest major generals, and he was given significant responsibilities as the Deputy Chief of Staff for Research and Development at Headquarters, Army Air Forces, in Washington, D.C. For two years, amidst a general military demobilization and the drive for air independence, he tried to stimulate development of new bomber and fighter technologies. He left Washington in October 1947 as a lieutenant general, assuming command of U.S. Air Forces, Europe (USAFE). LeMay was in Europe in June 1948 when the Soviets blockaded Berlin. A small, tentative military airlift began; within hours President Truman directed that it be expanded in size and scope. LeMay responded immediately; in addition, USAFE's forces went on combat alert. As the days of the Berlin Blockade grew into weeks, then months, tensions between the Soviet Union and the United States escalated. Anticipating war, Gen. Hoyt S. Vandenberg, Chief of Staff, USAF, and Stuart Symington, Secretary of the Air Force, surveyed the Air Force's combat capability. They judged the Strategic Air Command to be unprepared and ordered LeMay home to command the nation's strategic air forces. For the second time in four years, the Air Force had called upon LeMay to lead long-range strategic air forces. On both occasions, in World War II against Japan and in the Cold War against the Soviet Union, he had been given a similar mandate: reorganize and redirect an existing strategic air force so that American air power could influence the military situation directly.

LeMay began quickly. Within weeks he had replaced SAC's deputy commander, chief of staff, director of operations, and director of plans. The new men—Brigadier Generals Thomas S. Power, August W. Kissner, John B. Montgomery, and Walter S. Sweeney—were all veterans of the Pacific strategic bombing campaign. Experienced and confident, they began in the winter of 1948–49 to reshape the command, fitting together the people, aircraft, organization, training, tactics, and plans. As in the Pacific, LeMay was the driving force. Immediately, they changed training of air crews by instituting a lead crew school for elite bomb crews. Operational procedures were standardized by issuing new SAC manuals and checklists for operations, maintenance, supply, and support personnel. New, rigid unit rating systems pinpointed safety and held commanders accountable for aircraft accidents. Detailed, specific operational war plans were developed and tested in demanding operational training exercises. Gradually but perceptibly, a new combat attitude emerged at SAC; it was the product of the Cold War, LeMay, and the professional airmen reshaping the command.

When North Korea invaded South Korea in June 1950, President Truman and American military leaders believed that the invasion was a Soviet and Chinese Communist maneuver in the opening campaign of another global war. It was not. Yet it propelled the United States into the Korean War and, equally significant, into a massive rearmament program. The Strategic Air Command, as the nation's principal long-range retaliatory force, benefitted directly. It grew from 71,490 people and 868 aircraft in January 1950 to 170,892 people and 1,830 aircraft in December 1953. After the war ended in 1953, the expansion continued. President Eisenhower established a defense program that relied more on strategic air forces for deterrence and less on conventional ground and sea forces for projecting power overseas. The Air Force and SAC were the major beneficiaries as SAC modernized its bomber fleet, replacing propeller-driven B–29s and B–36s with new, all-jet B–47s, B–52s, and B–58s. SAC grew to 224,014 people and 2,711 aircraft by 1957, the year LeMay left the command to become Vice Chief of Staff, USAF. His legacy to SAC was the command itself: an American strategic air force that had become the dominant element in contemporary U.S. military strategy and the single most powerful military force in the history of war.

He remained at USAF Headquarters for eight years (1957–65), four as Vice Chief and four as Chief of Staff. During these years many of the Air Force's most significant issues concerned strategic forces. These included the acquisition and deployment of intercontinental ballistic missiles (Atlas, Titan, and Minuteman); continued modernization of manned bombers (B–58, B–70); standardization of all air refueling systems; evolution of advanced command control systems; development of satellites for reconnaissance, communications, and weather missions; and the establishment of a joint service strategic target planning agency. As Vice Chief, LeMay worked directly for Gen. Thomas D. White, Air Force Chief of Staff (1957–61), and with Gen. Nathan F. Twining, USAF, Chairman of the Joint Chiefs of Staff (1957–60). When General White retired in 1961, LeMay succeeded him. His tenure as Chief of Staff, coinciding with the Kennedy administration years, was turbulent and acrimonious. He clashed repeatedly with Secretary of Defense Robert S. McNamara and Chairman of the Joint Chiefs of Staff Gen. Maxwell Taylor. They differed on strategy, weapons, budgets, and people. Not only were their differences irreconcilable, but their resolution by McNamara and Taylor tended to downgrade the primacy of strategic nuclear forces in American military policy and strategy. Also in these years LeMay participated in the Cuban Missile Crisis (October 1962) and the early period of the Vietnam War (1961–65), both of which he discusses in this interview. In 1965 LeMay retired, having served the nation in uniform for thirty-seven years. Subsequently, he published his memoirs and in 1968 ran for Vice-President with Governor George C. Wallace of Alabama on the American Independent Party ticket. They lost and LeMay returned to private life, but true to his interest in air power and his concern for national defense, he has periodically visited Air Force installations and provided his judgments on issues of current concern.

General Johnson was born in Columbus, Missouri, in September 1904. He enrolled in the United States Military Academy at West Point in the summer of 1922, graduating in the upper half of his class. Commissioned a second lieutenant in the summer of 1926, he entered the Infantry, but shortly after completing basic training he transferred to the Army Air Corps. He never returned to the Infantry, serving the balance of his thirty-nine-year military career with air forces. During the 1930s Johnson served as an observation pilot at Mitchel Field, New York, and Nichols Field, Philippine Islands, spent an academic year at California Institute of Technology (Master of Science in Meteorology), held command and staff assignments in operational and support units, and attended the Air Corps Tactical School at Maxwell Field, Alabama. In September 1939 Germany invaded Poland and World War II began in Europe. In the thirteen years since his commissioning in 1926, Johnson had been promoted from second lieutenant to captain; in the next four he would rise from captain to brigadier general.

For most of World War II, the United States' preeminent strategic air force was the Eighth Air Force in Europe. Johnson flew and fought with the Eighth throughout the war, from its activation in January 1942 until victory in Europe in May 1945. The Eighth had only 24 officers and no aircraft when it went to England in April 1942. Three years and a month later in May 1945 it was the United States' and the Allies' largest and most powerful bomber command, with 171,022 people and 4,080 aircraft—2,646 bombers and 1,434 fighters. Johnson was one of the Eighth's first four flying officers, having responsibility for operations and training in early 1942. He went to Europe in June 1942, working as a staff officer directly for Maj. Gen. Ira C. Eaker, Commander, VIII Bomber Command. Although the first American bomb group arrived in England in July, the first strategic air strikes were not flown until mid-August. From that point forward into 1943, a new American bomb group arrived in England every few months. Initially, these inexperienced bomb groups fared poorly in combat: bombing accuracy was poor, navigation was inaccurate, and crew and aircraft losses were high. General Eaker, his staff, and group commanders established in the fall of 1942 an operational training school in England. Johnson, as the command's operations and training officer, had direct responsibility for starting and running this school. His successful leadership at the school led to his selection by General Eaker in January 1943 to command one of Eighth Air Force's first combat groups outfitted with B–24 Liberators: the 44th Bomb Group.

In the winter and spring months of 1943, Colonel Johnson's 44th Bomb Group experienced perhaps the roughest time of any unit in the Eighth Air Force. The 44th had arrived at Shipdham, England, in November 1942 with 27 B–24s and 90 crews. Over the next 7 months the group received a few replacement aircraft and crews, but despite these additions the group's combat losses were staggering: 20 B–24s lost in combat action and 7 damaged so severely as to be beyond repair. In one of the 44th's bomb squadrons, the 67th, 90 combat crewmen arrived at Shipdham in November; less than 10 were alive in May 1943. In that month replacement crews and aircraft arrived in sufficient numbers to reconstitute the group; shortly thereafter General Eaker sent Johnson's bomb group from England to North Africa for a special

Cadet Leon W. Johnson.
Courtesy Leon W. Johnson

strategic bombing mission. That mission was one of the most dangerous air strikes of the war: the Ploesti, Rumania, oil refinery raid. On August 1, 1943, the 44th flew, along with 5 other B–24 bomb groups (177 bombers), from Allied bases in North Africa across the Mediterranean Sea to Rumania where they navigated through heavy antiaircraft fire and enemy fighter defenses to strike the oil refineries. Johnson copiloted the group's lead bomber and led the formation over the target. So dangerous was this mission that 15 of the 17 B–24s in Johnson's formation failed to return to the landing base in North Africa. For the entire raid, 54 of the 177 B–24s were destroyed or damaged so severely they could not return; 522 men were killed or captured. Johnson and his crew hit the target and returned successfully to North Africa. For his leadership, courage, and heroism he won the Medal of Honor, one of five awarded that day.

Shortly after the Ploesti raid, Johnson became the commander of Eighth Air Force's 14th Combat Wing—a wing consisting of two, later four, groups of B–24s and B–17s. For the duration of the European war he led this wing, participating in every major bombing campaign: Central Europe, Normandy, Northern France, the Rhineland, Ardennes-Alsace, and Central Germany. As wing commander he led four distinguished bomb groups: the 44th, 392d, 491st, and 94th. Combined, the bombers and crews under Johnson's direction flew more than 15,000 combat sorties against the enemy. Combat hardened, knowledgeable about every aspect of strategic air warfare, Brigadier General Johnson emerged from the war as a leading practitioner of bomber operations and strategic air warfare.

Following the war, senior leaders of the Army Air Forces picked him to lead one of the two numbered air forces in the new Strategic Air Command. For eighteen months, 1947–48, he commanded SAC's Fifteenth Air Force, where he was responsible for leading, training, and equipping one element of the nation's small, atomic air force. It was a difficult assignment because postwar demobilization had created shortages of people, planes, equipment, and money in all of the Army Air Forces' combatant commands. In August 1948, Johnson left SAC for Europe where he commanded United States Air Forces Europe's Third Air Division. Activated in July 1948 during the first few tense weeks of the Berlin Airlift, this air division was based in England and had the dual mission of training and preparing the Air Force's strategic bombers in Europe for war and serving as a depot for the air transports flying the airlift.

For four years, 1948–52, during some of the most difficult moments of the Cold War, including the Berlin Airlift and the Korean War, Johnson trained and prepared American air forces in Europe for the possibility of war against the Soviet Union. Then in February 1952, Major General Johnson returned to the United States to lead the Air Force's Continental Air Command, a composite command of Air National Guard and Air Force Reserve forces. Three years later, he was tapped for a significant staff assignment. Like all of the military services in the postwar years, the Air Force made some of its most talented senior leaders available for national and international policy positions. A consequence of the United States' leadership role in the free world, especially in coordinating the North Atlantic Treaty Alliance (NATO), these positions called for a combination of military, political, and diplomatic experience. In succession, General Johnson served as the Air Force Member, Military Staff Commission, United Nations (1955), and United States Representative, North Atlantic Military Commission, NATO (1955–58). In April 1958, he became the Air Deputy, Supreme Allied Command, Europe. His final European duty started and ended with a significant international crisis. In 1958 Johnson helped direct the successful Lebanon intervention, and in 1961 he witnessed the Soviet-directed construction of the Berlin Wall. With the wall under construction and Cold War tensions at fever pitch, General Johnson returned to Washington and became the Assistant, then Chairman, of the Net Evaluation Subcommittee, National Security Council. In this key advisory position during the Kennedy and Johnson administrations, he participated in decisions affecting the Cuban Missile Crisis and the Vietnam War. In April 1965 he retired, completing thirty-nine years of military service.

A native of Pennsylvania and the son of a lawyer, General David A. Burchinal was born in April 1915. He attended Brown University, graduating with Phi Beta Kappa honors in June 1938. The rise of Hitler's Germany caused him to consider, like so many men of his generation, national military service. For Burchinal, this sense of patriotism was linked to the pure adventure of flying; in June 1939 he joined the Army Air Corps. A natural pilot, he advanced quickly from student pilot to instructor, then to depot test pilot. He flew everything and at one point in 1941 he was current in, or checked out to fly, twenty-nine different types of aircraft—trainers, fighters, bombers, transports, and experimental planes. Partly because of this proficiency, in July 1941, he became pilot and aide to Brig. Gen. Henry J. F. Miller, Commander, Air Technical Service Command, the forerunner of the USAF's Logistics Command. When General Miller was reassigned to Europe in early 1943, Burchinal did not accompany him; instead he went to the 330th Bomb Group, a B–24 unit bound for Europe, but then in training at Alamagordo, New Mexico.

Burchinal's arrival in New Mexico was instructive: traveling by train, he disembarked at the tiny Alamagordo station and was greeted by a staff officer standing amidst twenty wooden coffins—training fatalities for one week. The Army Air Forces expected pilots and crews to progress from single-engine to four-engine aircraft proficiency in ninety days. For some, that pace was simply too swift. As the group's operations and training officer, Burchinal instituted extensive night-flying training, stressed instrument flying, and placed instructor pilots in the tower twenty-four hours a day to reassure the nervous, inexperienced bomber crews. Gradually, confidence returned and accidents declined. "All those kids really wanted to know," he recalled later, "was the secret, so that they could go to war and come back home alive."

Burchinal, however, did not go to Europe with the 330th. Instead, in January 1944 he went to the 313th Bomb Wing, a B–29 outfit then in training for the Pacific. For eleven months they trained stateside. Then in December 1944, they left Nebraska with Burchinal piloting the lead bomber of the wing's 180 B–29s. When the wing arrived at Tinian Island in the Marianas, they joined the XXI Bomber Command, led by General LeMay. Burchinal flew several bombing missions immediately and participated in one of the first test raids on Japanese cities using incendiary bombs. By chance more than design, he flew the lead bomber of 231 B–29s on an early incendiary raid to Tokyo on February 25, 1945. The success of this strike led to the decision to conduct a series of low-level, night, fire raids on Japanese cities—Tokyo, Kobe, Nagoya, Osaka, and Kawasaki. Burchinal did not fly on these later

Lt. Col. David A. Burchinal.

missions, however, as General LeMay had him transferred to headquarters to be an operations planner. Unrelated but nearly coincidental was LeMay's decision to step up significantly the strategic air attacks on Japan. Additional strikes were ordered and LeMay instituted a series of new air tactics: repeated, low-level, night attacks on Japanese cities using incendiary bombs; increased spacing in the strings of B–29s flying over Japan so as to allow for flexibility in striking alternate targets; use of B–29 reconnaissance aircraft equipped with air-to-air radios for redirecting the bombers to strike alternate targets when over Japan; and later, in mid-summer 1945, the use of squadron-sized raids, instead of massed formations, to attack targets throughout the length and breadth of Japan. For Burchinal, these new tactics signaled that victory was near. Resistance to this air campaign was minimal. Burchinal recalled that every B–29 squadron was throwing its maximum effort against virtually every Japanese city. Japanese harbors and sea lanes were being mined and blockaded. Recalling those times, he remembered thinking then that if the Japanese could defend neither the airspace over their cities nor the sea lanes to their ports, their resistance could not continue indefinitely.

The Japanese government surrendered in September 1945. Unlike most of his fellow airmen, Burchinal did not return to the United States immediately. Instead, he joined the Strategic Bombing Survey, spending eight months studying how the economic, military, and political infrastructure of

Japan disintegrated under the combined effects of strategic bombing and the naval blockade. Following this analytical work, he accompanied Maj. Gen. Orvil A. Anderson, AAF, to Montgomery, Alabama, where he joined Air University's initial faculty. Teaching in the Air Strategy Division, he had the unusual opportunity of traveling extensively, since he and one other officer had responsibility for organizing the Air Force's first worldwide commanders' conference. They visited every command, briefed senior air leaders, and conducted the meeting at Maxwell AFB, Alabama, in 1949. This gathering became the model for subsequent worldwide commanders' conferences.

For Burchinal, the decade of the 1950s was seminal: air assignments working directly for senior air leaders; command of SAC bomb wings; promotion to general officer; and, finally, assignment to a major staff position on the Joint Chiefs of Staff. In April 1951, Gen. Muir S. Fairchild, Air Force Vice Chief of Staff, selected Burchinal to be the first secretary of the newly created Air Force Council. Composed of the Chief of Staff's five principal deputies, the council met frequently and recommended action on matters of policy and resource allocation throughout the service. Burchinal's job was to brief each issue and record the council's recommendations to the Chief of Staff. This council, like the worldwide commanders' conferences, became a permanent fixture in the Air Force. In April 1953, Burchinal left Washington for Kansas, assuming command of SAC's 40th Bomb Wing (B–29s) at Smokey Hill AFB. His timing was excellent; SAC's forces were being modernized, converting from long-range propeller-driven B–29s, B–50s, and B–36s to all-jet, refuelable B–47s and B–52s. Eight months after joining SAC, Burchinal was selected by General LeMay to command a B–47 wing, the 43d Bomb Wing, which had a distinguished combat record. Successful, he was promoted to general officer and reassigned as the Chief of Staff, Eighth Air Force. The Eighth's mission was to plan, prepare, and train for launching strategic air forces from bases located in the northeast and central United States against the Soviet Union in case of war. In 1958 Burchinal left SAC, becoming the Deputy Director, J–3 (Operations), for the Joint Chiefs of Staff. This assignment began an eight-year period, 1958–66, of senior staff positions with the JCS and USAF Headquarters.

In August 1962 Burchinal left the JCS and went to work for General LeMay, then Chief of Staff of the Air Force, as his Deputy Chief of Staff for Plans and Programs. Six months later Lt. Gen. Burchinal became Deputy Chief of Staff for Plans and Operations, the principal deputate for formulating operational plans at USAF Headquarters and the key Air Force officer on policy issues to the Joint Chiefs of Staff. Culminating these Pentagon years, Burchinal became in early 1964 the Director of the Joint Staff, Joint Chiefs of

Staff. He worked directly for Gen. Earle Wheeler, Chairman of the JCS. Just as the Vietnam War was expanding in 1965–66, Burchinal left Washington for Europe, becoming Deputy Commander in Chief, U.S. European Command. After nearly seven years in this position, one of the longest tenures of any American general, General Burchinal retired in 1972. He had served the Air Force and nation for thirty-four years.

A native of southern California, General Jack J. Catton was born in 1920. Athletically inclined, he enrolled in Loyola University of Los Angeles on a football scholarship in September 1939; that same month Hitler sent the German Army into Poland, beginning World War II in Europe. Catton's athletic career lasted but one season; the war lasted for six years, and Catton's participation in it propelled him into a military career spanning thirty-four years. Catton's decision to enter the military was based, in part, on the advice of his father, a successful southern California businessman. Late in 1939 Catton's father, in a discussion about the future with Jack Fry, Vice-President of Trans World Airlines, concluded that the best way for a young man to become successful in the soon-to-be burgeoning aircraft industry was to enroll in one of the military flying schools, complete pilot training, and then return to California and enter a growing corporation. In May 1940, Catton followed this advice and entered the Army Air Corps as a flying cadet. He progressed quickly through primary and advanced flying schools at Santa Maria, California, and Randolph and Kelly Fields, Texas. Commissioned in February 1941, he was immediately caught up in America's military expansion. As a trained pilot he was called upon to teach flying to the hundreds, then thousands, of the Army Air Forces' flying cadets. From January 1942 to April 1944, Catton instructed AAF pilots and crews in advanced training schools for B–17 bombers, amassing 2,500 flying hours himself. He worked hard, rising from second lieutenant to major in three years. Yet, he wanted to fly in combat.

In April 1944 he joined the 73d Bomb Wing (B–29s), then in training, but slated to deploy in September to the Pacific. An excellent pilot, Catton was selected by Brig. Gen. Haywood S. Hansell, Jr., Commander, XXI Bomber Command, to fly the lead B–29 from the United States to the Marianas. Once there, Catton flew the lead aircraft on the wing's first long-range mission to Tokyo on November 24, 1944. From then until the surrender of Japan in September 1945, he remained in the Marianas, flying or working on the commander's operational staff. In the spring of 1945, Catton left the cockpit temporarily to become an operations planner at the command headquarters. Maj. Gen. Curtis LeMay had replaced General Hansell, and the command was preparing to unleash a sustained, low-level night campaign using incendiary bombs against major Japanese cities. Working with Maj. David Burchinal, Lt. Col. William H. Blanchard, Col. John B. Montgomery, and others, Catton's job was to brief the day's mission to LeMay and his senior staff. Daily they met, going over each specific mission, reviewing the appropriate air tactics, bombing patterns, rescue techniques, communication procedures, and the coordination routines established with Allied naval forces. Like other Army Air Forces airmen who fought in the war, Catton learned the art of piecing together an air campaign by working under pressure as an operational staff officer. Those experiences transformed him from a citizen-airman who had become a top-rated bomber pilot into a professional career officer. When the war ended, a future in the postwar air force seemed a certainty to the twenty-five-year-old lieutenant colonel.

The first twelve months after the war confirmed that conclusion. Following a brief encounter with notoriety as an actor in a documentary film on the strategic air war against Japan, Catton became in January 1946, Director of Tactics, 444th Bomb Group, Tucson, Arizona. Barely a month into that job he and his B–29 crew were selected as a lead crew in Air Task Group 1.5, a special composite AAF unit then preparing for atomic weapons tests in the Pacific. Designated Operation CROSSROADS, these 1946 tests involved some 42,000 Army and Navy people and measured the effects of atomic weapons on naval warfare. Seventy-three captured Japanese and German vessels were anchored at Bikini Atoll in the Pacific where two atomic bombs were detonated on July 1 and 25, 1946. Catton and his crew flew their B–29 over the bomb sites and recorded the weapons' effects. This direct experience with atomic weapons, when coupled with his time working with General LeMay in the Pacific war, placed Catton in a very small cadre of air officers who were both knowledgeable and experienced enough to build the nation's incipient atomic air force. In March 1946, the Strategic Air Command was established; in August, following the CROSSROADS tests, Catton was selected to command SAC's 65th Bomb Squadron (B–29s). One year later he went back to the Pacific, leading Task Unit 741 in Air Task Group 7, which was another composite force participating in the large joint Navy-Army-Atomic Energy Commission atomic tests in the Pacific. Returning to SAC in May 1948, Catton progressed through operational wing assignments to a position as an operational planner at Headquarters, Strategic Air Command. He was working at headquarters on October 19, 1948, the day Lt. Gen. Curtis LeMay arrived.

General LeMay would lead SAC for the next nine years (1948–57); Lt. Col. Catton would remain in SAC for the next sixteen (1948–64). He was one of LeMay's ablest field-grade officers, holding command and staff positions in bomb wings, air divisions, numbered air forces, and command headquarters.

Maj. Jack J. Catton presents briefing at XXI Bomber Command in the Marianas. Courtesy Jack J. Catton

He rose from lieutenant colonel to major general. In one six-year stretch (1958–64), Catton served as chief of staff for Eighth Air Force and commanded the 817th, 822d, 823d, and 821st Air Divisions. Yet, this seemingly inexorable rise in rank and responsibility had one major period of despair that very nearly aborted his career. On Labor Day, 1951, he was diagnosed as having polio, the crippling disease which, if severe enough, could have paralyzed him for life. After hospitalization, physical therapy, and rest, he was able to return to a desk job. Encouraged by senior officers, Catton resumed flying. His flying skills had not diminished and, as his strength returned, he moved into command positions.

After more than a decade and a half in the Strategic Air Command, Maj. Gen. Catton left that command and went to Air Force Headquarters in 1964 as the Director of Operational Requirements in the deputate of the Deputy Chief of Staff for Programs and Resources. General LeMay was Chief of Staff, General Burchinal was Deputy Chief of Staff for Plans and Programs, and General Johnson was Chairman of the Net Evaluation Subcommittee, National Security Council. Three years later, Lt. Gen. Catton became the Deputy Chief of Staff for Programs and Resources at Headquarters, Air Force. In 1968 General Catton returned to the operational Air Force, commanding first SAC's Fifteenth Air Force (1968–69), and then the Air Force's Military Airlift Command (1969–72). At the time the Military

16

Airlift Command was a worldwide force of 86,174 people and 766 aircraft. During General Catton's tenure, the command increased its airlift capacity with the introduction of the first C–5A operational wing, which was used to transport American military forces and equipment to and from Southeast Asia. In 1972 General Catton left MAC and assumed command of the Air Force Logistics Command. Following two years as the service's chief logistician, he retired in 1974, completing 34 years of military service.

Strategic Air Warfare

Participants	Active Duty Years
Gen. Curtis E. LeMay, USAF, Retired	1928–65
Gen. Leon W. Johnson, USAF, Retired	1926–65
Gen. David A. Burchinal, USAF, Retired	1939–73
Gen. Jack J. Catton, USAF, Retired	1940–74
Dr. Richard H. Kohn, Chief, Office of Air Force History	

Preparations for World War II

Kohn: We are very pleased that you four gentlemen have taken the time to return to Washington after the Senior Statesmen Conference. Let us start with the 1930s and follow the historical development of the strategic air forces and the Air Force experience with strategic air warfare.

My first question concerns the extent to which we were prepared for the strategic bombing campaign in World War II. Apparently, the Army Air Corps changed from a tactical to a strategic air force in the 1930s. Do you have any sense, General Johnson or General LeMay, when and why this occurred, and how the transformation into a strategic air force occurred?

LeMay: Well, I don't think it happened until the 1940s. At the end of World War I we had realized the potential of bombardment. But we didn't have any bombers, *per se*; our first bombers were DH–4s, two-seater airplanes that had bombs hung on the wings.[1] You couldn't carry any load or really have much chance of doing too much damage, but you could see the potential. In the

---

[1] In World War I U.S. Army Air Service leaders selected the British-designed de Havilland 4 (DH–4) as its standard combat aircraft. After the war, they continued using the DH–4, while revising its performance characteristics with newer models. In 1923–24 Boeing manufactured the DH–4M, which had an improved, welded steel-tube fuselage along with the reliable Liberty engine. This model was in service until the early 1930s. It had a 1,288-pound bomb capacity. See F. Gordon Swanborough and Peter M. Bowers, *United States Military Aircraft Since 1909* (London, 1963), 196–203.

1930s that potential was realized to some extent. We finally built some bombers such as the B–1s and –2s, or bigger biplanes, that would carry heavier loads.[2] But they were slow, clumsy, ninety-mile-an-hour things. I think the big push came when we got the first monoplane, which gave us a tremendous leap forward in performance. As a matter of fact, at the beginning of the decade we had bombers that would go faster than fighters. That leap forward gave great impetus to the bombing end of the picture and began to fulfill our earlier expectations. I don't think there was any stress on the bombers over the fighters; we had attack airplanes and observation airplanes also. However, we never had enough airplanes to call it a strategic air force.

Burchinal: Those bombers were Martin B–10s, weren't they?[3]

LeMay: Yes. There was no radical change in theory or roles but a big jump in the performance of bomber equipment.

Johnson: Personally, I don't think we had a sense of mission early in the 1930s. The world had been made safe for democracy not too long before, and there seemed no chance of a war. We weren't conscious of Hitler. I happened to be in the Philippines during those times, and we had a bomb squadron, a fighter squadron, an observation squadron, and a pursuit squadron over there.

We flew around the islands and did our training because that's what you did in peacetime. I know that we didn't have a sense of purpose at that time. We didn't see anything on the horizon; we weren't worried about anything. We were just worried about getting enough airplanes to fly, and we were worried about getting our flying done. I quite agree with you that when the long-range fighter came in and Seversky made his P–35, then they began to say, "Well, there is a possibility of moving, and you can take these forces

---

[2] The B–1/Keystone and B–2/Curtiss Condor bombers were acquired by the U.S. Army Air Corps in the late 1920s and early 1930s. The Air Corps purchased 140 of these aircraft and they became first-line bombers until the mid-1930s. Both aircraft had technological improvements over the DH–4s. Both were biplanes that had maximum speeds of 120–130 miles per hour, ranges of 700–800 miles, and bomb load capacities of 2,500 pounds. Swanborough and Bowers, *United States Military Aircraft Since 1909*, 277–281.

[3] Martin B–10s were all-metal, monoplane bombers that became operational in the Army Air Corps in 1934. They represented significant technological advances in aircraft design and performance. These bombers had two engines, all-metal frames, retractable landing gear, a maximum speed of 210 miles per hour, a range of 1,240 miles, and a bomb capacity of 2,260 pounds. They could fly faster and higher than any Air Corps' pursuit or fighter aircraft. Because of these characteristics, air power advocates within the Army pushed for a larger role for strategic bombers in American defense policy. See Swanborough and Bowers, *United States Military Aircraft Since 1909*, 330–333; John F. Shiner, *Foulois and the U.S. Army Air Corps, 1931–1935* (Washington, 1983), 50–51

different places."[4] You [Gen. LeMay] were up in those Great Lakes maneuvers in 1931?[5] I know I was up there.

LeMay: Yes.

Johnson: It was just flying a formation around to show the people we had airplanes.

LeMay: We really didn't have an air force. We were an Air Corps, part of the Army. I didn't know it at the time—I was at Selfridge Field in Michigan in the 1930s—and about all we got done up there was to open up airports. That was the mission assigned up there. The battle for an air force was on; we were getting nothing in the Air Corps in the way of appropriations for new equipment to make any progress toward our goal. It was a matter of educating the people and the country to the potential of air power in order to try to do something about the budget. That was practically the mission at the time: to educate the people. So we opened airports all over the place and flew demonstrations and things of that sort. It was more like a flying club than a military organization. True, we had a little bit of gunnery here and there, but day-to-day we had no emphasis on tactics or preparing to fight an air war. It was almost like a public relations outfit; that's what it amounted to, throughout the air force.

As Leon says, overseas—in the Philippines, Hawaii, and Panama—we would have a squadron of bombers, a squadron of fighters, and some observation airplanes. We did have a squadron of attack aircraft over in Hawaii. We may have had that in the Philippines. But the basic doctrine was that we would have the bombers and the fighters to escort them, and we

---

[4] Alexander P. de Seversky (1894–1974) was a World War I Russian military air ace and aeronautical engineer who emigrated to the United States during the Russian Revolution of 1917. In the 1920s he was a test pilot for the U.S. Air Service where he worked on special aeronautical projects for Brig. Gen. William Mitchell. Later he founded a small aircraft manufacturing company in California, and by the mid-1930s de Seversky had achieved a reputation as an aircraft designer. The P–35 was a small monoplane with an enclosed cockpit. It had a maximum speed of 290 miles per hour and a range of 950 miles. The U.S. Army Air Corps purchased 77 P–35s and 60 P35As in 1935–36 from de Seversky's company, which reorganized in 1937 and became Republic Aviation. In 1938 de Seversky designed and built a turbo-charged, air-cooled, experimental fighter which became the P–47 Thunderbolt. During World War II, Republic built a total of 15,579 P–47s.

[5] The Air Corps maneuvers of May 1931 were led by Brig. Gen. Benjamin D. Foulois, Assistant Chief of the Air Corps, who organized a provisional air division (670 aircraft). With this air division, the Air Corps tested the air arm's capability to deploy a large force from Wright Field in Dayton, Ohio, to several large midwestern and eastern cities: Chicago, Cleveland, Pittsburgh, and New York. While most of the flying involved aerial demonstrations over the cities, these maneuvers did test the Air Corps' logistics and safety procedures. Judged on that basis, the maneuvers were successful. The 670 aircraft flew 37,000 hours without any serious accidents. See Shiner, *Foulois and the U.S. Army Air Corps*, 34–40.

21

would also have the attack airplanes to go in ahead and work over the antiaircraft. That was the general theory. All of the historians and writers now point out the fact it was a big surprise to us when we got over to Europe in the war and found that the bombers had to have fighter escort. It was no surprise; we always expected to have fighter escorts. The only trouble was, we didn't have any fighters, and we had long since abolished the attack airplane, so we didn't have any of them either.

Kohn: Was there not a theory, at the time, that unescorted bombers could make it through to the target if you arranged them properly and armed them sufficiently?[6]

Brig. Gen. Haywood S. Hansell (left) and Col. Curtis E. LeMay, Commander of the 305th Bomb Group, in front of a Boeing B–17.

---

[6] In the 1930s this theory was discussed and taught at the Army Air Corps Tactical School at Maxwell Field, Alabama. There, a small, influential group of officers on the faculty, led by Maj. Harold L. George, Maj. Donald Wilson, 1st Lt. Kenneth L. Walker, and 2d Lt. Haywood S. Hansell, Jr., developed a set of concepts about air power. They believed that air power could directly influence the course of wars by having strategic air forces fly long-range missions and destroy an enemy's industrial infrastructure. Further, they taught that these long-range bombers, if properly equipped with defensive armament and organized into massed formations, would be capable of penetrating an enemy's defenses and striking directly at the enemy's will to resist. As the decade of the 1930s progressed, these teachings developed into an unoffical doctrine of air power that became prominent in World War II. For fuller explanations of these men and their theories of air power, see Robert T. Finney, *History of the Air Corps Tactical School 1920–1940* (Maxwell AFB, Ala., 1955); Thomas S. Greer, *et al.*, *The Development of Air Doctrine in the Army Air Corps, 1917–1941* (Maxwell AFB, Ala.,1971); Robert F. Futrell, *Ideas, Concepts, and Doctrine: A History of Basic Thinking in the United States Air Force, 1907–1964* (Maxwell AFB, Ala., 1971); and Haywood S. Hansell, Jr., *The Strategic Air War Against Germany and Japan: A Memoir* (Washington, 1987).

LeMay: Speaking generally, I don't think many ever believed that was the way to do it. We had to do some unescorted missions if we were going to do any bombing at all. It could be done, yes. On the first Schweinfurt mission, for instance, I flew clear across Germany without any fighter escort and destroyed a target. But you paid a price for it.[7]

Schweinfurt left in flames as Flying Fortress departs.

---

[7] Several major American strategic air raids in the summer and fall of 1943 persuaded AAF leaders that the bombers had to have fighter escorts if they were to fly deep into Germany on a continuing basis. On the Ploesti, Rumania, raid of August 1, 1943, 177 B–24s attacked the Eastern European oil refineries and did limited damage, but suffered losses of 54 bombers and 532 men. The strike against Regensburg, Germany, on August 17, 1943, used 146 B–17s to assault the Messerschmitt fighter aircraft factory, with some success, but with losses of 24 aircraft and 240 men. The raid on Schweinfurt, Germany, also on August 17, 1943, saw 230 B–17s hit the ball bearing plants, with a loss of 36 aircraft and 360 crewmen. In one day, Eighth Air Force had lost 60 aircraft, which was 19 percent of the striking force. Finally, on October 14, 1943, 291 B–17s struck Schweinfurt in a second massed attack. While the aircraft manufacturing plants were damaged, Eighth Air Force lost 60 bombers and 600 men and sustained damage to 138 returning B–17s. So severe were these losses that Eighth Air Force did not return again to Germany until January 1944. The Schweinfurt-Regensburg raids have long been considered milestones in the strategic air war, when American airmen decided that daylight raids into Germany had to await development and employment of long-range fighter escorts. Wesley F. Craven and James L. Cate, eds., *The Army Air Forces in World War II*, 7 vols (Chicago, 1948–1956; reprint, Washington, 1983), II, 684–690, 696–706, 848–850; Kenneth P. Werrell, "The Strategic Bombing of Germany in World War II: Costs and Accomplishments," *Journal of American History* 73 (December 1986): 702–713.

Johnson: I don't doubt that was one of the most hazardous missions in the whole war. Those Schweinfurt missions were unbelievable. I know that I was fortunate enough to receive the Medal of Honor for fifteen minutes of fighting, over Ploesti, and they fought for about five hours over Schweinfurt. I don't remember anyone getting a Medal of Honor out of that. I think I would rather do five Ploesti raids than one Schweinfurt.[8]

Burchinal: I think a major reason why the Royal Air Force went at night was because they could keep their losses down to acceptable levels by operating in the dark.

LeMay: The British drifted into that. They started out in daytime, but they didn't have the proper equipment. The Wellington bomber, for instance, had .30-caliber guns and it wasn't as well defended as our B–17s.[9] Their loss rate rose so high that they were forced into night bombing. Then they concentrated on night bombing and built their equipment for it, whereas we started out bombing in daylight with better equipment for the purpose.[10] But we didn't have the fighters we needed built yet.

---

[8] For a brief account of Johnson's actions in the Ploesti, Rumania, raid, see Introduction, p 9. Three histories of the raid are James Dugan and Carol Stewart, *Ploesti* (New York, 1962); Leon Wolff, *Low Level Mission* (New York, 1957); and Leroy W. Newby, *Target Ploesti: View From the Bombsight* (Novato, Calif., 1983).

[9] Wellington medium-range bombers flew in the RAF's first strike against Germany, hitting Wilhelmshaven on September 4, 1939. The Wellingtons, first produced by Vickers in 1936, had a maximum speed of 255 mph at 14,000 feet and a range of 1,325 miles. Early in the war these RAF medium bombers were armed with six .30-caliber machineguns—two in the nose and four in the tail turret. This defensive armament did not afford protection from above, below, or either side. On early missions to the continent, German fighters caused considerable losses. By contrast, the B–17 possessed the heaviest armament of any Allied bomber early in the war. The B–17 had eight .50-caliber machineguns mounted in the nose, tail, turrets above and below the fuselage (both were power-operated, rotating twin .50-cal. guns), and, later, two "chin" guns forward of the cockpit. Kenneth G. Munson, *Aircraft of World War Two* (New York, 1962), 43, 152.

[10] In 1942–43 American and British air leaders disagreed on the proper method for employing strategic air forces against Germany. Initially, American air leaders planned to use heavily armed, long-range bombers equipped with gyroscope-controlled bombsights to carry out massed daylight strikes against specific targets in Germany. Consequently, the American war plan specified a force structure of strategic bombers—first, B–17s and B–24s, then B–29s and B–36s, which would be massed at high altitudes to carry out the precision bombing campaign. The British Royal Air Force, relying on the operational experiences learned in 1939–41, adopted a strategic bombing campaign based on a stream of bombers flying at night and striking "areas" rather than precise targets. When the American bomber forces went to England in July-August 1942, the issue of daylight or night, precision or area bombing tactics, was discussed by American and British military and political leaders. However, while the discussions were significant it is far more important to recognize that the general concept of employing strategic air forces against Germany had been settled—Allied strategic air forces would carry the war to Germany in the long months before the invasion and liberation of the continent. Not until January 1944 were long-range fighters (P–47s, P–51s) available in quantity in Europe. These fighters escorted the American bombers into Germany and fought an intense, sustained, and

Catton: Of course, you had the advantage of high altitude and greatly improved defensive armament on the B–17, which permitted you to attack in the daylight. The other point which is obvious, of course, is that the bombers out-ranged the fighters, so that the fighters could not make the long haul with the bombers. As General LeMay says—and I am just affirming—nobody *wanted* to go without fighters. When we started operating out of the Marianas, for example, and out of India-China against Japan, we didn't have any fighters that could go with us. We would have loved to have had them, and as soon as we could, we got them, and used them.

Johnson: At first, in Europe we thought we could handle the enemy's fighters better than we did. We handled them quite well until they started those nose attacks on our formation and came through, breaking up the formation. I remember very well we were going to do a mission down to Bordeaux, and I asked, "How many fighters are there?" Intelligence had predicted twenty-five. I said, "Oh, we can handle those all right," because the enemy hadn't had much experience. We had no trouble with them.[11] But those yellow-nosed babies over there learned how to go through our formations, they would break us up, and we were in real trouble then.

LeMay: Another weakness of ours right from the start was our horrible gunnery. Gunnery was pretty low on the totem pole in peacetime. You never could get enough ammunition. I remember down at Langley Field before the war everybody shot skeet. When that was cut out, I gathered up all the old skeet ammunition. Then I had the gunners fire the then-standard flexible gunnery course. I took them to the skeet range and shot up all the ammunition I had accumulated over a period of months. Then I ran them through the gunnery course again. They increased their scores by 300 percent. But did that make any difference and did we get our skeet

---

ultimately successful air battle against the German Air Force in the spring of 1944. See John Terraine, *A Time For Courage: The Royal Air Force in the European War, 1939–1945* (New York, 1985), 471–472, 542–545; R. J. Overy, *The Air War 1939–1945* (New York, 1981), 139–141; Kent Roberts Greenfield, *American Strategy in World War II: A Reconsideration* (Baltimore, 1963), 85–122; Williamson Murray, *Strategy for Defeat: The Luftwaffe 1933–1945* (Maxwell AFB, Ala., 1983), 321–326, 166–173; DeWitt S. Copp, *Forged in Fire: Strategy and Decisions in the Air War over Europe 1940–1945* (New York, 1982), 145–147, 212–220, 263–265; Ronald Schaffer, *Wings of Judgment: American Bombing in World War II* (New York, 1985), 20–34, 60–106.

[11] This Bordeaux mission took place on May 17, 1948, when 198 American B–24s and B–17s flew from England along the Atlantic coast of France and bombed German U-boat facilities and the ports in Bordeaux and L'Orient. Met by German fighters, the bombers kept in formation and flew straight over the ports and U-boat basin dropping their bombs successfully on the target. The 10 bomb groups that flew on this strike lost 6 B–17s, 1 B–24, and 69 crew members. Roger Freeman, *Mighty Eighth War Diary* (New York, 1981), 60.

ammunition back? No. Gunnery was the last thing you did because you were at peace and ammunition cost money, and there wasn't any money. So our gunnery was terrible. We had no airplanes to train with, and nobody knew how to shoot well enough to train our people. We were just terrible. We raised such a fuss about it over in England in 1942 that the commanders at the six or seven AAF gunnery schools were sent over to see what all the fuss was about. We sent all of them out on a combat mission, and on their first mission four of them got shot down. That emphasized our point.

Burchinal: The equipment was relatively primitive, too. You stood at the open waist of a B–17 at 24,000 feet, freezing, with an oxygen mask and all the heavy winter equipment on—just an open bay—with no computing sights or anything like that.

Johnson: Also, the pressure was on the training commands to get us crews; people were sent over who weren't trained. I can't say positively, and I am not sure I should say it at all, but I talked to a number of crews that had never been to altitude, really, and yet they came through all checked off as having completed training.

LeMay: Some had never been in an airplane. The gunners I got came supposedly from a gunnery school, but they had never been in an airplane. They had used a flexible gun, mounted on a truck, that they would run up in front of a dirt bank out on the prairie someplace and shoot into the bank. I got my gunners one ride in an airplane, shooting at the desert as you ran across at low altitude. That was it; then we went into combat.[12]

Burchinal: I was at the training end at that point back in the United States and I remember the ninety-day wonders. We took those kids out of single-engine flying school, and ninety days later, we sent them in a four-engine bomber over to England, thinking they were going to be able to fly in combat. There were three stages of thirty days each and "on your way." Before that you had to have 3,000 hours and fifteen years of experience as a pilot before you could fly the B–17.

LeMay: The pilots that I got weren't even ninety-day wonders. They came right from flying school and single-engine airplanes, and they had never been

---

[12] In the first year of the Army Air Forces' participation in the war (1941–42), AAF gunnery schools trained 12,161 men. These schools lacked adequate planes, turrets, trainers, cameras, bomb sights, and qualified instructors. See Craven and Cate, *AAF in WWII*, VI, 471–72. For a more extensive discussion of General LeMay's experiences in England early in World War II, see Curtis E. LeMay and McKinley Kantor, *Mission With LeMay* (New York, 1965), 197–238; Thomas M. Coffey, *Iron Eagle: The Turbulent Life of General Curtis LeMay* (New York, 1986), 25–26.

in a multi-engine airplane until I got them in the 305th. We used three old beat-up B–17s to train crews. About all I got accomplished was to check them out so they could get up and get back on the ground without cracking up. We never flew formation until we got to England. The practice formation on the first day after we got there was a complete debacle. The next day I got them up, and on the radio got them positioned the way I wanted them. The third time we flew, we flew across the Channel.[13]

Catton: General LeMay, the first B–17 school as you know—the Training Command School—started in Sebring, Florida, at Hendricks Field in February 1942. That was the first time we were generating relatively well-trained combat crews for B–17s, and the demands from the United Kingdom were horrendous.

Burchinal: We produced airplanes faster than we did crews.

Johnson: One of the worst features of gunnery early in the game was that the guns froze at altitude. They had no oil that would take the low temperatures up there, so the machineguns froze up at altitude. But we corrected that. I think it took about a month to do it.

LeMay: We corrected it by washing the guns in gasoline before we put them in. You had to stand around with a club to do that, because all the gunners thought, "Just a little bit of oil on there won't hurt it." But the oil would freeze up. We finally learned to wash all the oil off when you assembled the guns for a mission.

Burchinal: Dry guns.

---

[13] LeMay commanded the 305th Bomb Group that arrived in Chelveston, England, in September 1942. A B–17 outfit, the 305th gained a reputation for tactical innovation, based largely on LeMay's interest in bomber tactics and concern for rigorous training. Disappointed in the bomb group's initial missions over the continent during which most of the B–17 crews failed to drop bombs accurately and showed a lack of air discipline, LeMay began experimenting with tactical formations. Rather quickly he settled on a staggered three-element combat box formation with eighteen bombers in the "box." The group's three six-plane squadrons were then positioned in a lead-high-low wedge-shaped formation. This arrangement (see illustration) gave the group a compact, yet maneuverable, "box-like" formation. On the bombing run LeMay ordered his pilots, navigators, and bombardiers to concentrate on the lead aircraft and to fly straight and level over the target. At this time accepted air tactics called for the bombers to maneuver every few seconds over the target to avoid enemy antiaircraft fire. LeMay rejected this conventional wisdom and told his bomb group to concentrate on placing "bombs on target." Using these tactics, the 305th was able to achieve air discipline *and* bombing accuracy. In the fall and winter months of 1942, the command's wing commanders recognized the 305th's results, and they—specifically, Brig. Gen. Laurence Kuter, and Brig. Gen. Haywood S. Hansell, Jr.—recommended that LeMay's air tactics be adopted in all Eighth Air Force bomb groups and wings. They were. Roger A. Freeman, *The Mighty Eighth: A History of the U.S. Eighth Army Air Forces* (New York, 1970), 22–23, 247; Craven and Cate, *AAF in WWII*, II, 264–267.

STRATEGIC AIR WARFARE

Kohn: Could I go back to the 1930s for just one moment to ask a question about doctrine? Did you ever read Giulio Douhet's *Command of the Air* ?[14] Did you ever discuss the theory of strategic bombing, or how the force would be used in wartime, even though you didn't have an enemy and weren't looking forward to a war?

Johnson: Individually we all had heard of Douhet, and we talked about Douhet, but I don't think we paid that much attention to theory. The airplane could only do certain things, and we all believed in the airplane. We had the airplanes, and we thought we could do the job. The Tactical School[15] and schools over in England were a bit of a disappointment to me when I went to them. I went to the short course only at Maxwell. Before that time most of us hadn't gotten to school. I thought when I got to England the instructors were going to have all the answers. When I got there they didn't have any more answers than we had. They were groping, too.

LeMay: I feel about the same way. I never saw a copy of Douhet's book. I had heard about him and that he generally favored the use of air power and what it could do. We agreed with that. Of course, we had Billy Mitchell,[16] and we knew more about his battle for air power, and we knew about the bombing of the German ships off the Virginia Capes and so forth. There wasn't much question about what we could do if we had something to do it with.

Kohn: So the theory was always there. It was pretty generally understood that

---

[14] Giulio Douhet (1869–1930) was an Italian military officer and theorist who authored a treatise on air power, *The Command of the Air*, first published in 1921. Douhet's work was one of the most influential theoretical statements on air power. His writings were translated into French, Russian, German, and English and discussed in military schools and institutions.

[15] The Army Air Corps Tactical School was located at Maxwell Field, Alabama, during the 1930s. Usually, Air Corps officers attended the 14-week school at the midpoint of their careers. Both Capt. Leon Johnson and 1st Lt. Curtis LeMay attended the school from May to August 1939.

[16] Brig. Gen. William Mitchell (1879–1936) led the U.S. Army Air Service's combat forces in Europe in World War I. In the 1920s he was an outspoken advocate for an independent air force, separate from the Army. In articles and speeches he attacked the Navy as well, asserting that the airplane had rendered the battleship obsolete. In a 1921 exercise, and again in 1923, Mitchell had Air Service pilots locate, bomb, and sink captured German warships. Amidst tumultuous publicity, Mitchell used the sinkings to push for military air independence. In 1925, when a Navy dirigible was lost with its entire crew in a severe storm at sea, Mitchell chastised the Navy and War Department for "incompetency, criminal negligence, and an almost treasonable administration of national defense . . . ." For these assertions he was court-martialed and convicted of insubordination in a sensational trial. He resigned from the Army in February 1926. Until his death in 1936, Mitchell continued publicizing his airpower concepts in books and articles, including *Winged Defense* (New York, 1925), and *Skyways, A Book on Modern Aeronautics* (New York, 1930). For an excellent biography, see Alfred F. Hurley, *Billy Mitchell: Crusader For Airpower*, 2d ed. (Bloomington, Ind., 1975).

the great value of air power would be the strategic role if you had the airplanes and the capabilities. Of course, you had to fight the Army, and . . .

Burchinal: It wasn't that well formulated.

Johnson: We knew if we had airplanes that could go someplace, we could take them there and hopefully bring them back. I think that was understood by all of us, and that the airplanes could bomb.

Burchinal: This was theory, but there was a minimum of doctrine, really. Doctrine was not formulated, not thought through, not put down. It was just there.

LeMay: I got that short course at the Tactical School, too, and I found that most of it was 180 degrees off from the facts of life out where the lead was flying around. For instance, we fought an air battle in an exercise with the ground troops at Gettysburg. I remember another problem we had off Florida. The only thing we had was a group of fighters to attack an invading force. More than half of us expended the fighters on that attack, which kind of surprised the instructors down there because we had to make the attack beyond the range of the fighters and we sent them out there knowing they weren't coming back. I think we all had the general idea of what had to be done, but we didn't have the tools.

Air Corps Tactical School Students of 1939: Capt. Leon Johnson is 6th from the left in the 2nd row and 1st Lt. Curtis Lemay is the 6th from the left in the 3rd row. Courtesy Leon W. Johnson

29

Johnson: I am not sure we reasoned things through well enough. I remember one problem at the Tactical School: how to handle submarines off the coast. I made a fairly good grade on the thing. I sent all the airplanes down to South America, and on the trip down, they hit everything in the ocean and then gassed up over-night and came back and hit everything on the way back.

General LeMay, early in the war you took a mission, I think, to North Africa, and it took four days to get back to England.

LeMay: We made plenty of advanced plans for that shuttle mission down to Africa in 1943. I went down personally and talked to General Spaatz,[17] and Spaatz, of course, shuffled me off to Norstad.[18] So I gave Norstad all the dope. "Where am I going to land down here, I asked?" He said, "Well, you land at Telergma. That's a depot. There will be mechanics and spare parts and all the help you need." So I said, "All right, that's fine, but I don't trust the communications. You keep your eyes open, and the first day the weather is good deep in Germany, we will be down there. If you don't get any messages on it, don't be surprised." We had to scrub the mission once, and it was a month before we actually flew the mission. In the meantime the war had marched on, and when we landed at Telergma, there wasn't a damn thing

---

[17] Gen. Carl Spaatz (1891–1974).   Educated at West Point and respected before the war by senior Army and Army Air Forces leaders, Spaatz served as Commander, Eighth Air Force (May-July 1942); Commander, U.S. Army Air Forces in Europe (July 1942-Feb 1943); Commander, Allied Northwest African Air Forces, and Commander, U.S. Twelfth Air Force (Feb 1943-Dec 1943); Commander, U.S. Strategic Air Forces in Europe (Jan 1944-July 1945); and Commander, U.S. Strategic Air Forces in the Pacific (July 1945-Sept 1945). General Eisenhower ranked Spaatz with Bradley as his ablest generals of the entire war. In 1946, General Arnold retired and General Spaatz became Commanding General of the Army Air Forces. When the Air Force became a separate service in 1947, President Truman named Spaatz as its first Chief of Staff. See Alfred Goldberg, "Spaatz," in *The War Lords: Military Commanders in the Twentieth Century*, ed. Sir Michael Carver (Boston, 1976), 568–581; David R. Mets, "Carl Spaatz: A Model for Leadership?" and I.B. Holley, "General Carl Spaatz and the Art of Command," in *Air Leadership: Proceedings of a Conference at Bolling Air Force Base, April 13–14, 1984*, ed. Wayne Thompson, (Washington, 1986), 3–14, 15–37.

[18] Gen. Lauris Norstad (1907–88). A West Pointer, Norstad was a brilliant young air officer who became the trusted confidant of General Arnold in World War II. In October 1942 Norstad went to North Africa, serving as the Assistant Chief of Staff for Operations, Mediterranean Allied Air Forces. Within six months he was promoted to brigadier general and made Director of Operations. As such, Norstad directed tactical air operations, including airfield assignments for aircraft entering the North African theater. As the war progressed, General Arnold brought Norstad back to Washington where he became Chief of Staff, Twentieth Air Force. This air force had responsibility for all strategic air operations against Japan, including the atomic bombing mission which ended the war. In the years after the war, Norstad was one of the architects of the independent Air Force. In 1956 General Norstad became the Supreme Allied Commander, Europe (SACEUR), the allied command coordinating the military forces of the nations in the North Atlantic Treaty Organization. He retired in 1963, after completing thirty-three years of military service.

there except about a dozen enlisted men, a detachment with no spare parts, no mechanics, no nothing. But we got back to England in about four days.[19]

Johnson: That's the problem. It sounds so simple on paper; it sounds so right, but it doesn't work out that way.

World War II: Europe

Kohn: What kind of modifications did you have to make that first year or two when you got to Europe? You now had the planes, you were there, and you knew what you wanted to do. You have talked in the past, General LeMay, about having to modify the tactics of actual bombing. Few people had experience; I suppose yours was the same experience, General Johnson?

Johnson: No, I hadn't had as much in bombers. I had medium bomber experience, the B–18. We were practicing bombing with B–18s. I had been in attack fighters and then went into B–18s and A–20s, but I had not been in heavy bombardment.[20]

---

[19] The mission of August 17, 1943, was the largest United States air strike of World War II to that date. Known as the Schweinfurt-Regensburg raid, it was the deepest penetration of Germany and involved 376 B–17s and 108 B–24s. It provoked an intense, fiercely fought air battle over Germany: German Air Force fighters, flak, and rockets shot down 60 and damaged 168 B–17s and 22 B–24s. General LeMay commanded the 3d Bomb Division and flew the lead B–17 over Regensburg and bombed the Messerschmitt aircraft factory. His division, equipped with long-range fuel tanks, then flew south across the Alps to North Africa, landing in a dust storm at Telergma and Bone airfields, Algeria. General Hap Arnold had great expectations for this long flight pattern—England to Germany to North Africa—hoping to take advantage of the better weather in the Mediterranean for launching return missions over Europe. These return strikes, Arnold thought, would confuse the German air defense systems. But LeMay dashed Arnold's hopes when he reported from North Africa that the maintenance and living facilities were insufficient, operating conditions poor, and crew morale uniformly poor. As a result of LeMay's counsel, no further such flights were conducted by Eighth Air Force. See Craven and Cate, *AAF in WWII*, III, 681–687; Freeman, *The Mighty Eighth*, 67–70.

[20] The terms light, medium, and heavy bomber were widely used in the 1930s to denote the bomb capacity and mission of the Air Corps' bomber force. The B–18, for instance, was a twin-engine, medium bomber with a maximum speed of 215 miles per hour, a range of 1,200 miles, and a bomb capacity of 6,500 pounds. This bomber was modeled on the famous Douglas DC–3, and after 1935 it replaced the B–10 as the Air Corps' standard bomber. The Air Corps acquired 350 B–18s between 1935 and 1940. The A–20 was a twin-engine, light attack bomber produced by Douglas in the late 1930s. It had a speed of 347 miles per hour, a range of 670 miles, and a bomb load of 2,600 pounds. Because it was in production before the war, A–20s were acquired by the British, French, Dutch, and American air forces. The designation of heavy bomber was reserved for the B–17, B–24, and B–29 bombers, which were four-engine, long-range, strategic bombers. See Swanborough and Bowers, *U.S. Military Aircraft Since 1909*, 74–83, 84–90, 218–220, 230–236.

LeMay: I don't think we had to make any change in tactics in England; there weren't any tactics there when we started, because there wasn't anybody there who knew anything about it. There wasn't even a wing headquarters that could write a five-paragraph field order. That's one thing I did learn down at the Tactical School: how to write a field order. I had to go up there and tell them about the five-paragraph field order so we could get some sense out of this ten feet of teletype paper that came down with the mission for the next day. They didn't even know those basics, much less anything about tactics. Everybody was learning the business from the ground up.

Johnson: The expansion was so great that it was almost impossible to imagine that we were over there with groups already fighting.

Kohn: So you went out and tried whatever you would think might work, and when you came back, you would assess it and make whatever changes were necessary to get the bombs on the target?

Johnson: That's an overstatement, I think. We had a pretty good idea that things were going to work unless you hit too much opposition.

Burchinal: But you started and sort of fought your way into the railroad yards at Lille and St. Omer; the ones that were just across the Channel. The initial operations were just across the Channel, really.[21]

LeMay: That's right.

---

[21] The first mission of Eighth Air Force was flown on July 4, 1942, from England across the channel to strike at German airfields in Holland. For the remainder of the year, American B–17 and B–24 missions to the continent were characterized by small numbers, short distances, and limited damage to the enemy. The bombing mission to Lille, France, on October 9, 1942, was typical. Early in the morning the Eighth dispatched 108 B–17s and B–24s to attack railroad yards and industrial areas. First, the bombers of the 97th, 301st, 92d, 306th, and 93d Bomb Groups formed up over England and began their flight across the channel. Then, three P–38 fighter squadrons joined the bombers at mid-channel and escorted them to the target and back. En route, 29 bombers turned back because of mechanical or crew problems. The remaining 79 bombers flew to Lille and dropped 16,700 pounds of high explosives on the steel mills and rail yards. The bombing pattern was poor, with many bombs falling outside of the target area and causing many civilian casualties. Over the city, the German Air Force attacked the American bomber formation with FW190 fighters, but their successes were few, shooting down but one B–17, damaging another, and damaging 10 B–24s. Despite American bombers' defensive skills in fending off the German fighters, the mission had glaring problems. Inexperienced crews contributed to the bombing inaccuracies, and the performance of the B–24s was very poor. Of the 24 B–24s that started from bases in England, 14 turned back for mechanical reasons, and the 10 that reached Lille were shot up badly. When Lt. John Stewart, for example, landed his B–24, named *Bomerang*, it had more than 200 bullet holes in its fuselage and wings. His ground crew chief, M/Sgt Charles A. Chambers, took one look and said: "Goddamit Lieutenant—What the hell have you been doin' to my ship!" Freeman, *The Mighty Eighth*, 18–19.

Burchinal: And then operations developed as you went deeper from there.

Kohn: Were there surprises about the defenses? Did the Germans surprise us either with the amount of their flak or the positioning of it or the nature of their fighter opposition?

LeMay: I wasn't surprised, particularly. No.

Johnson: I wasn't surprised at all. I did not have any respect for flak for quite awhile. When I went to North Africa on loan in 1943, and I said, "How many fighters are down here?" They replied, "There are not many fighters, but a lot of flak." I said, "The hell with the flak; we can take that. It won't bother us." But it got heavy enough that it did bother us. It was the fighters that I didn't like anyway, because they learned how to handle the formations.[22]

LeMay: I felt the same way. One of the things I heard was a story from Frank Armstrong[23] that ten seconds in a straight line of flak and they would shoot you down; that didn't sound right to me, since I had taken field artillery in ROTC at Ohio State. For some reason or another, I had a field artillery manual in my footlocker that I had sent over with the ground echelon. I got that out and sat down and worked out a precision fire problem with the French 75mm gun, which we were equipped with in ROTC, (and which was comparable to the German 88mm antiaircraft guns).[24] I found out

---

[22] Johnson went to North Africa in June 1943 as the Commander, 44th Bomb Group, Eighth Air Force.

[23] Lt. Gen. Frank A. Armstrong (1902–69). During World War II Armstrong led the first American B–17 bombing attacks on continental Europe. The first strike occurred on August 17, 1942, when Col. Armstrong led 12 B–17s of the 97th Bomb Group, Eighth Air Force, to Rouen, France, and bombed the railroad marshalling yards. For this successful operation he received a silver star, distinguished flying cross, and the British flying cross. An advocate of strategic bombing in the 1930s, Armstrong had been Eighth Bomber Command's first operations officer, and had commanded its first combat-ready bomb group. Within the Army Air Forces he was considered an expert on strategic bombing operations. Early in 1942 he wrote the first training manual for B–17 and B–24 crews preparing to go to the European theater. In February 1943, Armstrong became a general officer, and for the duration of the war he led American strategic bomber wings in Europe and the Pacific. After the war he commanded air defense, strategic, and theater air forces before becoming in 1956, Commander, Alaskan Air Forces.

[24] The French 75mm gun, model 1897, was the finest, and most widely used Allied field artillery piece of World War I. During that war the U.S. Army adopted the French gun as its field gun, and in the interwar years the Army used it extensively. The model 1897 75mm gun could fire a 14.7 pound shell a range of 37,500 feet. The 88mm antiaircraft guns, issued initially in 1934, were standard for Germany in World War II; they projected 20-pound, armor-piercing shells at a rate of 15–20 per minute up to a height of 32,500 feet.

it took 300 rounds or something—I have forgotten, some big number—to hit a B–17 sitting on the hillside 25,000 yards away. That didn't sound too bad to me. In my stupidity, not knowing any better, I said, "We are going to make a straight-in run from the time we see the target until we drop the bombs off." We are going to get a bomb run, and we did. At the end of the run, we went right over the target and got the pictures, and then I took the airplane off automatic pilot and got out of there. I asked the bombardier how he did. He said, "Well, we hit the target, but I would have done better if it wasn't for the clouds." There was not a cloud in the sky; we were flying through pretty heavy flak. But we didn't lose any airplanes. From then on we did it that way.

Kohn: And your accuracy improved.

Typical Eighth Air Force heavy bomber group complement, as shown for Chelveston, May 10, 1943:		
Unit	*Officers*	*Enlisted*
Hq 305th Bomb Group	18	36
364th Bomb Squadron	59	316
365th Bomb Squadron	55	317
366th Bomb Squadron	60	310
422d Bomb Squadron	57	313
Hq & Hq Sqdn 325th Service Gp (less detachment)	17	85
343d Service Sqdn	6	205
1121st Quartermaster Company Service Group (less detachment)	1	35
876th Chemical Company (less detachment)	1	40
1632d Ordnance Maintenance Company (Aviation)	2	38
Detachment A, 983d MP Company Aviation	3	49
Detachment 105, 18th Weather Sqdn	2	7
8th Station Gas Defense Detachment (P)	0	4
Detachment B, Hq & Hq Sqdn 304th Service Group (Finance)	1	7
	282	1762

Source: Roger Freeman, *Mighty Eighth War Manual* (New York, 1984), 131

LeMay: We got accuracy where they didn't have any at all before. Actually, when you figured it out with the accuracy of an artillery piece, the enemy was firing up at you and the quicker you got through where he could shoot at you, the less rounds could be fired at you, and the less chance by the laws of probability of being hit. If you weaved around, you stayed in the vulnerable area longer. It was actually better to go straight through. We just ignored flak—I did—right from the very start.

We had an antiaircraft artillery officer in our division headquarters, and every time we had a mission he had all the intelligence information out and all the guns plotted around the target. He could tell you that if you came in this way, you were going to have so many rounds fired at you, and if you came in over here, you were going to have so many rounds. The Germans knew how to lay out a defense, and it didn't make any difference from an artillery standpoint which way you came in. So we generally picked an approach with the sun at our back, or some other good approach. If a nice road ran down to the target, that was fine; it helped the crews get in and find the target. That was how we did it, not paying any attention to the artillery. We would fly right through it and come home. The fighters bothered me more than anything else, mainly because I had been in fighters for seven years, and seeing those guns winking at me out there bothered me, whereas the flak didn't.

Actually it is no great shakes to shoot a bomber down with a fighter if you go in there and press the attack. Of course, with all that lead flying around, it was not conducive to long life and happiness, but the fighters that did it shot bombers down.

Catton: General LeMay, can you identify a period of time when the crews that you received in the UK were well trained?

LeMay: That never happened.

Catton: I knew you would say that.

LeMay: We established a combat crew replacement center in England where we gave the men a little more training; things were moving so fast that the Training Command never caught up. Certain of the later groups were better than the ones we started with, of course. But we always had to sort of "break them in" a little bit, try to baby them a little bit, and give them an easy mission to start with. We broke them in that way. Without exception, every time a new group went into combat, they usually screwed up the first mission.

Kohn: Was your experience similar to that, General Johnson?

Johnson: I have said many times I never saw a mission in World War II that

35

went off the way it was briefed. I thought it depended very much on the leadership and who was leading it. Always, something different occurred, something you had not expected.

Kohn: General LeMay told me last night that he never agreed with the frag order as it came down from wing when he was in the group. He was always calling back up and arguing with the folks. Was that only in the first year or two, only in 1942, General LeMay?

LeMay: To start off with, yes I argued. Then later on they got a little education down at Bomber Command, and it got a little bit better. They changed operations officers, and General Orvil Anderson came over.[25] Remember, Orvil supposedly was one of our top thinkers and tacticians in the Army Air Forces. He would run out the order, and as soon as he got it ready to go, he put it on the teletype, then went to bed just as we would begin getting it out in the outfits. I wouldn't like some of the things I saw. The colonel he left on duty down there wouldn't do anything about it, and I would finally have to go get Orvil out of bed and get some changes made. In other words it was a matter of education. Orvil's theory was fine, but he had no practical experience. He hadn't been there, and it was only natural that he missed a lot of things.

Kohn: Was your experience similar to that, General Johnson?

Johnson: General LeMay was at a higher echelon than I was. We carried out the orders. We fussed about them sometimes and tried to get changes made, but they generally came down to us from the division, and we accepted them most of the time unless we had something we really wanted to change.

---

[25] Lt. Gen. Orvil A. Anderson (1895–1965). Early in the war Anderson was Assistant Chief of Staff for Plans, at AAF Headquarters. In the fall of 1942, General Arnold directed Anderson to set up an office that would compile and digest all of the data regarding strategic bombing operations and prepare reports for the President, JCS, Chief of Naval Operations, and the Congress. As head of this office, Anderson became familiar with all aspects of Eighth Air Force operations in Europe. Then, in February 1943, he went to Europe where he became Chairman of the Combined Operational Planning Committee, an Allied committee with representatives from RAF Bomber Command, RAF Fighter Command, Eighth Air Force, VIII Bomber Command, and VIII Fighter Command. This committee was responsible for coordinating tactical plans for specific Allied combined bombing operations. While it was an advisory body, the committee did rule on the feasibility of specific bombing missions; thus, it had to know the technical and operational dimensions of strategic air warfare. At the end of the war General Anderson served on both the European and Pacific strategic bombing surveys that evaluated the bombing campaigns. In the postwar years, Anderson served as Commandant, Air War College, from 1946 to 1950.

Kohn: When the Ploesti order came down and when that planning was revealed to you, what was your first reaction to it?[26]

Johnson: I see you are implying that I was opposed to it. I don't remember being opposed to the mission; I was opposed to going in at low altitude. We were right at the peak of our high-altitude bombing training. We had done one or two good missions just before that up in England, and we thought we could do it from altitude and not take the losses. We knew—I had been in attack fighters for years—that anybody can hit an airplane going in at treetop level, even with a rock if he throws it at the right place. So we knew we could be knocked down. We thought we were at the peak of bombing training. We wrote a letter to Gen. Brereton trying to get the orders changed, but he said that it would take a campaign to destroy Ploesti at altitude, which it did a year later, and that we didn't have the airplanes for a sustained campaign.[27] All we could afford was one mission, and we would do it at low level. So we did it.

Kohn: Was it difficult to motivate the crews because of that change in tactics? Was it a leadership rather than a . . .

Johnson: No, no question. The crews wanted to look up to their commanders. Good Lord, their lives depended on their commander! I never saw crews that

---

[26] Air planners had long been interested in oil: destroy the enemy's oil refineries, and its armies, navies, and air forces could not fight. Intelligence sources had estimated that 60 percent of Germany's oil was being produced at the Ploesti, Rumania, oil refineries. Consequently, Army Air Forces planners devised a mission that would fly from Allied airfields in North Africa across the Mediterranean and Yugoslavia to Rumania where it would destroy the refineries. It was to be a single mission, with a massed formation of heavy bombers (177) flying at low level and traversing 2,000 miles from start to finish. For an account of the plan and its execution, see Dugan and Stewart, *Ploesti*; Wolff, *Low Level Mission*; and Freeman, *The Mighty Eighth*, 86–91.

[27] Lt. Gen. Lewis H. Brereton (1890–1967). A graduate of the U.S. Naval Academy (1911), Brereton resigned his Navy commission and entered the U.S. Army Signal Corps prior to World War I. He became a pilot in 1916, flew combat in the war, and served on Brig. Gen. Mitchell's staff. In the interwar years Brereton commanded tactical, pursuit, bombardment, depot, and training units. At the beginning of World War II he was one of the Army Air Forces' senior air leaders. Immediately after the Japanese struck Pearl Harbor on December 7, 1941, Maj. Gen. Brereton, then Commander, Far East Air Forces, in the Philippines, was selected by Gen. Douglas MacArthur to be the Air Commander-in-Chief, Allied Air Forces, Pacific. During the next six months, Japanese forces engaged and defeated American and British forces throughout the western Pacific. With few forces and no hope of resupply, General Brereton was transferred, first to India in March 1942 to command Tenth Air Force, then to Egypt in June 1942 to lead the Middle East Air Forces, and finally to North Africa in November 1942 to command Ninth Air Force. Brereton commanded the forces that flew on the Ploesti Raid of August 1, 1943. Early in 1944, he was selected to command the 1st Allied Airborne Army and following the Normandy invasion he led this allied force for the balance of the war in Europe. After the war, Brereton served in Washington in the Office of the Secretary of War and on the Atomic Energy Commission's Military Liaison Committee. He retired in 1948.

didn't admire their commander unless he was a very poor stick. In Eighth Air Force I was based up in East Anglia, and I would drive down to London about once a month. I had an old seven-passenger Packard. And on the way down there, I would fill it up with people thumbing rides. I would ask them

B–24 Liberators enter target area in Ploesti at extremely low altitude against background of flame and smoke of burning fuel.

Lt. Gen. Jacob Devers (right) saluting Col. Leon Johnson, moments after he had placed the Congressional Medal of Honor around Johnson's neck, Shipdham, England, 1943. Courtesy Leon W. Johnson

what group they belonged to, and they always sang the praises of their commanders. Some of them I knew, and I didn't think they were as good as the men thought they were, but all of the men admired their commanders unless they had just lost one recently, or changed and they hadn't come yet to admire their new one. Crews want to look up to their commanders, the same way I want to look up to my President.

Burchinal: Of course, your crews hadn't been there before, either, at treetop level. You would always hope that was going to surprise them.

Johnson: After the mission was over, I went down to a little sergeant there, and he said, "Colonel, you practically lied to us." I said, "How did I lie to you?" He said, "You said it wasn't going to be bad." I replied, "I didn't say that; I said, 'I *hoped* it wasn't going to be bad.' "

Catton: There is an analogy to that, and it deserves more discussion later on—but as an anecdote I recall in March 1945 that we ran the first five low-level incendiary raids on Japan with the B–29s out of the Marianas. At that time I was still flying a lead crew up in Saipan. We finally had developed good lead crews. We went to the prebriefing that the lead crews got, and we came back and worked the problem out with our people in the squadron. My bombardier, a guy named "Porky" Canfield, commented, "Wait till you hear this; this will kill you." We were going in at 4,500 feet as the lead crew on Tokyo. We had never attacked below 24,000–25,000 feet before that time. Of course, it was a night operation, and an entirely different proposition than Ploesti—it was very successful.[28]

LeMay: We will get into the discussion as to why this happened later on.

Kohn: Before we shift to the Japanese campaign, let me ask what the four of you think was the major factor in our success in the strategic bombing of Germany? While we argue over a definition of success, historians generally believe that the bombing of Germany wrought tremendous havoc on the Germans, and that bombing contributed materially to ending the war and ending it more quickly. There has been a continuing dispute over the word "decisive," and controversy over the effectiveness of the campaign.

LeMay: The biggest factor was getting the airplanes over there necessary to do the job.

Kohn: Was it numbers, General LeMay?

LeMay: It was plain and simple numbers. There was no radical change in tactics or anything else. In the early days we just didn't have enough airplanes to do the job. All the writings you see of the failures of the Army Air Forces to prove Mitchell and Douhet correct are wrong. We simply did not have an air force there to do the job well. We did what fighting we could,

---

[28] The March 9–10, 1945, low-level, night fire raid on Tokyo signaled a major change in the strategic campaign against Japan. General LeMay, commanding XXI Bomber Command for about six weeks, had concluded that high-altitude, precision bombing was not succeeding because of poor weather and an unexpectedly fast jet stream over Japanese targets. According to historian James Lea Cate, LeMay's decision turned essentially on operational factors: not only the difficulties of wind and weather, but the inadequacy of the enemy's antiaircraft fire (two B–29s shot down in 2,148 sorties), the lack of Japanese night fighter units (only two according to intelligence), and LeMay's personal belief in the ability of the crews to fly the night missions successfully. But General LeMay was also under considerable pressure from Washington, where discussion of incendiary attacks had antedated the Pearl Harbor attack, where the use of fire had been studied extensively by staffs and experts for many months. Previously, small incendiary raids had been tried in late 1944 and early 1945, but the success of these tactics led, between March and August 1945, to a focus on incendiaries against urban targets in the rest of the campaign. In all, XXI Bomber Command's bombers dropped 147,000 tons of bombs and laid over 12,000 mines in Japanese waters; 66 cities were devastated, causing by the most recent estimates 900,000 deaths and perhaps 1,300,000 injuries, and forcing perhaps a fourth of Japan's urban population to evacuate the cities. Historian Cate noted that the change in operation concept and in tactics, and the subsequent campaign, "was to mark him [LeMay] as one of the very greatest operational air commanders of the war . . . ." See Craven and Cate, *AAF in WWII,* V, 608, 609–627, 754–755; Michael S. Sherry, *The Rise of American Air Power: The Creation of Armageddon* (New Haven, 1987), 58, 60, 101–102, 109, 112, 116, 220–233, 266–267, 269–282, 406n, 413n.

but we always had in the back of our minds to keep the loss rates down, not any more fighting than we could pay for, so that we would have an ever-increasing force, and someday out in the future, we would have a force large enough to do the job.[29]

When we finally got a force over there big enough to do the job, we were pulled off the strategic mission to help to prepare for the invasion. Thousands of sorties were directed against railyards and bridges and everything in order to isolate the battlefield to prepare for an invasion. Of course, we were pulled off on other chores, like sub pens, and trying to help win the Battle of the Atlantic, and things of that sort that were pressing matters.[30]

Johnson: On 3 January, 1943, I took over the 44th Bomb Group, and we didn't receive any replacement crews until late March or April. So we had a limited number of crews. Every time we went out, while we might lose none, we might lose one or two. At dinner that night over at the club, there would be vacant seats. It was awfully hard. You didn't have to be very smart to figure out that if your force was going down all the time and you were doing the same number of missions and you were losing one and two and getting no replacements, your chances of surviving didn't look so good.[31]

---

[29] American bombers (light, medium, and heavy) and bomb tonnage in the European Theater in World War II were:

	Bombers in Theater	Combat Sorties *	Bomb Tonnage *
(Jan-May)			
1942	607	9,749	4,964
1943	3,514	233,523	97,937
1944	7,904	1,012,101	683,605
1945	6,977	438,192	310,288

* Figures are totals for all U.S. combat aircraft in European Theater, 1942–1945.

Source: Office of Statistical Control, *Army Air Forces Statistical Digest of World War II* (Washington, 1945), 156, 220, 242.

[30] Accounts of the allied strategic air war in Europe can be found in Craven and Cate, *AAF in WWII*, I, II, III; Charles K. Webster and Noble Frankland, *The Strategic Air Offensive against Germany, 1939–1945*, 4 vols, (London, 1961); Noble Frankland, *The Bombing Offensive against Germany* (London, 1965); Anthony Verrier, *The Bombing Offensive* (London, 1968); Max Hastings, *Bomber Command* (New York, 1979); Terraine, *A Time for Courage*.

[31] Johnson commanded the 44th Bomb Group, the "Flying Eightballs," from January 3 to September 2, 1943. It was the first Eighth Air Force group equipped with B–24 Liberator bombers. During the winter and spring months of 1943, the 44th lost in combat 20 of its original force of 27 B–24s and had another 7 damaged so severely as to be declared as beyond repair. Not until April 1943 did replacement aircraft and crews arrive in England. Even with this infusion of new people and planes, the loss rate among crews was so high that the bomb group lacked experienced pilots, navigators, and bombardiers. Of the 90 crewmen, for instance, who arrived in England in November 1942 with the groups's 67th Bomb Squadron, less than ten remained in mid-May. See Freeman, *The Mighty Eighth*, 36–39.

LeMay: I can give you one more experience. I had the 305th Bomb Group—this was about the spring of 1943. We were all pretty flat. We had been working hard, no sleep, and so forth. Everybody was just tired out, and then all at once, "bang," everything was back to normal again. I didn't figure out what happened for two or three months: the crews could do simple arithmetic, and at the rates we were losing crews and getting replacements, the last B–17 would go off on a mission 30 days later. The men had concluded, "We are not going to make it. We might as well get shot down today as tomorrow; let's go." It was that simple.

Johnson: As soon as the replacement crews started arriving, there were no problems at all. I don't mean to say that there were problems earlier, but you could see it in their eyes and their whole manner. Everybody did the calculations, and they knew that their chances weren't very good. When the new crews came in, it changed completely.[32]

B–17s and fighter escort enroute to European mainland.

---

[32] In mid-April 1943, four new B–17 bomb groups—the 94th, 95th, 96th, and 351st—arrived in England to augment the six American bomb groups already engaged in the Eighth Air Force's strategic bombing campaign. In early May another two groups, one a reequipped and the other a remanned older unit, joined the command. Thus, within one month in late spring 1943 the number of bombers and crews in Eighth Air Force doubled, easing the pressures on the crews. Maj. Gen. Ira Eaker, Commanding General, Eighth Air Force, wrote General Arnold, "our combat crew availability went up in a straight line from 100 to 215." See Craven and Cate, *AAF in WWII*, III, 338.

I was anxious to have support—fighter escort—and Fred Anderson was over at Bomber Command at the time, and he visited the group.[33] I said, "Fred, you have got to get us some support." He said, "Oh, we will fly all over Europe without any fighter escort." I didn't remember saying it to him, really, but the next year he was over, and he said, "I told you we would fly over Europe without any escort." Well, we did, of course, but we paid the price. The issue was, how much of a price were you willing to pay? I then started arguing and said, "Well, we wasted these missions." Yet, we won the war. Which mission was wasted? I can't say any one of them was wasted. They all accumulated to the point that we did win and probably at a much lower cost than if we had to invade under different circumstances.

Burchinal: Did you recognize that the quality of the German Air Force deteriorated from attrition—loss of pilots and all—and that the Germans weren't as effective as they had been?

LeMay: Yes. We knew their effectiveness was going down. For instance, when they started shooting those missiles at us, if their crews had been a little better trained, if they had come in a little bit sooner with sights for the missiles, it would have been a different picture.[34] If the crews had been a little more experienced, it probably would have been a different picture. You could tell the difference in the quality of German pilots.

---

[33] Maj. Gen. Frederick L. Anderson (1905–69) was a graduate of West Point (1928) and an early convert to strategic bombing. As a second lieutenant, Anderson decided to devote his career to studying and learning about strategic air warfare. In the 1930s he flew and worked in the 2d Bombardment Group with Maj. George E. Stratemeyer, Capt. Clarence L. Tinker, and 1st Lt. Kenneth N. Walker. When the war came, Anderson helped organize the expansion of bomber training in the United States. He went to Europe in May 1943 and commanded a new bomb wing, the 4th Bombardment Wing, Eighth Air Force. This wing embraced the 94th, 95th, and 96th Bomb Groups (96 B–17s). From May 1943 to May 1945, Anderson participated in every major bombing campaign of the European war. During the war, he rose to command Eighth Air Force's VIII Bomber Command. Maj. Gen. Anderson retired in 1947, and during the Eisenhower administration served as the U.S. Ambassador to NATO (1952–53).

[34] During the summer of 1943 the German Air Force refined its fighter tactics against the massed formations of Allied bombers. The Germans began using large formations of fighters, which attacked the Allied bombers first by firing rockets at a range of 1,000 to 1,700 yards into the rear of the bomber formations. Then the German fighters shot off explosive cannon shells and sent air-to-air bombs into the formations. Finally, they concentrated their forces and attacked directly at specific three-plane elements of the Allied formations. During the week of October 7–14, 1943, the Germans used all of these tactics and weapons and shot down 148 American bombers and approximately 1,500 air crewmen. Although the American losses were severe, so too were the Germans who lost hundreds of fighters and pilots. During the late summer of 1943 the air war over Western Europe had become a war of attrition. Between July and October 1943 the American Eighth Air Force lost or "wrote off" 454 bombers, the RAF Bomber Command lost 813 aircraft, and the German Air Force lost 1,229 fighters. See Murray, *Strategy For Defeat*, 169–176; Craven and Cate, *AAF in WWII*, 696–706.

Johnson: I noticed later on that we never saw fighters. At first our fighters escorted the bombers. Then we got enough fighters to hit their bases and destroy their planes. So while the bomber crews didn't feel comfortable not seeing our fighters, we came back with a lot fewer losses because our fighters were beating up their airdromes.

LeMay: There were crews that went through their twenty-five missions without even seeing a fighter.

Burchinal: We got a help from Goering, too, and Hitler, when they stood down the −209a and didn't push through with the −262s.[35]

LeMay: That helped. The −262 would have made a difference if they had gotten a quantity of them there. The time came when Doolittle did release the fighters from escort duty to more beating up of the countryside.

Burchinal: And it worked, really.

LeMay: There weren't enough enemy fighters then to make much difference. We had a mass of bombers, so we could go without fighter escort without an exorbitant loss rate.

Johnson: Curt, I am going to put in one thing about the loss rates. We have talked about milk runs, easy missions. You never knew which were easy missions. We attacked Foggia, Italy, one day in 1943 when we were in North Africa. I never saw any enemy aircraft as we flew from North Africa to Italy. About two weeks later we went back up there, and we lost eight airplanes. The Germans had fallen back out of Sicily, and they were defending Foggia at

---

[35] Historians have believed that the Luftwaffe's defeat was due to several factors: unwarranted German optimism after the quick military victories over Poland, Holland, Belgium, and France in 1939–40; German failure to anticipate the need for full industrial mobilization until 1941–42; the pressure of the Allies' Combined Bomber Offensive against Germany and the German Air Force in 1943–45; and finally, the poor leadership of the German Air Force by Adolf Hitler, Hermann Goering, Ernst Udet and the top command of the Luftwaffe. See Murray, *Strategy for Defeat*, 299–319. The Me–209, designed by Willy Messerschmitt, was a second generation, twin-engine, fighter-bomber which was beset with production difficulties until Reichs Marshal Goering canceled the project in April 1942. Instead, he pushed for production of the Me–262, a twin-engine, turbojet fighter, then under development. However, the Me–262 was plagued by technical, administrative, production, and political delays. So few of the German jet fighters ever flew in combat that scholars estimate that they had little impact on the sustained air battle that raged over Germany. Murray, *Strategy For Defeat*, 252–253; R. J. Overy, "The Military and the European Economy 1939–1945," *Militärgeschichtliche Mitteilungen* (March 1979), 55–78; Walter J. Boyne, *Messerschmitt Me 262* (Washington, 1982).

that time; yet we had put in new crews and had told them, "This is a milk run."[36]

Burchinal: Was it by late 1943 that air fighter opposition had fallen off?

LeMay: It was after D-day in 1944. We had spent so much time isolating the Normandy battlefield. We had beaten up all the airfields, or our fighters had beaten them up, and we had hit some with the bombers. Their oil supply was pretty well down at the time, too. So they just didn't have it.

There was absolutely no air opposition at all at the Normandy invasion.[37] I think I heard once that two Me–109s got in and made a pass at the beach. That was all. There was no other air activity. The Germans just didn't have it, couldn't get it there.

Johnson: To go back to the issue of the effectiveness of the strategic campaign, I must say that there are only certain things you can do with airplanes. You don't have to be a genius to know that if you knock out an enemy's oil, he can't fly. But I think we were spattering our shots; it seems to me that when I was in operations with Spaatz in 1942, we had just too many targets on our list. You would just get started on one target system and say, "Oh, the fighters are starting to build up. You have got to hit these factories." And then the loss of shipping in the Atlantic would capture our attention— 600,000 tons in one month, I remember. Then it would be said, "Hit the submarine pens." You would just get started on one little program— something would happen—and you would have to change your targets.

LeMay: Airmen weren't running the air war. We were under the theater

---

[36] On July 15, 1943, Ninth Air Force B–24s attacked the German fighter air base at Foggia, Italy, with little opposition. When 86 B–24 Liberators returned to strike the same base a month later on August 16th, they were met by approximately 100 German and Italian fighters. See Kit C. Carson and Robert Mueller, *The Army Air Forces in World War II: Combat Chronology 1941–1945* (Washington, 1973), 158, 175.

[37] In June 6, 1944, the U.S. Army Air Forces sent 8,722 aircraft over France in support of the Normandy Invasion. The British Royal Air Force launched another 4,115 aircraft that same day. Flying a variety of missions—reconnaissance, airlift, air superiority, close air support, interdiction, and area bombing—Allied air forces dominated the sky, losing only 127 aircraft to enemy fire. The German Air Force did not interfere with the Allies' landings on the Normandy beaches. By the end of D-day more than 150,000 troops were on French soil, preparing to move inland. See Carlo D'Este, *Decision in Normandy* (New York, 1983), 95, 116, 146–147; Max Hastings, *Overlord: D-day and the Battle for Normandy* (New York, 1984), 244–276; and Richard H. Kohn and Joseph P. Harahan, eds., *Air Interdiction in World War II, Korea, and Vietnam: An Interview with Gen. Earle E. Partridge, Gen. Jacob E. Smart, and Gen. John W. Vogt, Jr.* (Washington, 1986), 23–29.

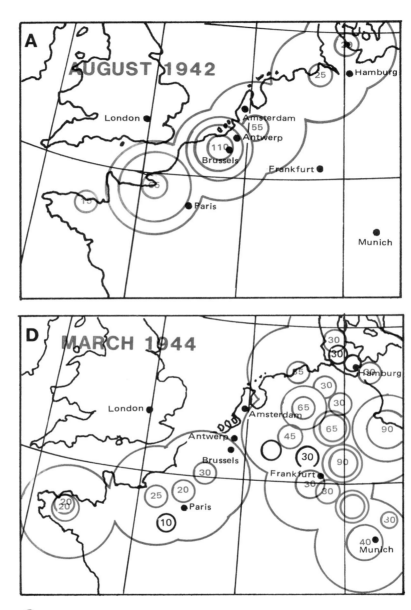

A

AUGUST 1942

London

Amsterdam
55
Antwerp
110
Brussels
Frankfurt

Hamburg
25

Paris

Munich

D

MARCH 1944

30
30
Hamburg
30
65
30
London
Amsterdam
65
65
45
90
Antwerp
30
Brussels
30
Frankfurt
90
20
20
25
20
30
10
Paris
40
Munich

○ Single-Engine Day Fighters
○ Single-Engine Night Fighters
○ Twin-Engine Day Fighters

Source: Eighth Air Force and Army Air Forces Evaluation Board, *Eighth Air Force Tactical Development, August 1942-May 1945*, 1945.

commander, and he determined what the first priority would be at any given time. If we had just concentrated on the oil, and the synthetic oil to start with, it would have been a big help. We did make a feeble attempt on the ball bearings, and we did get that. However, the Germans got ball bearings from Sweden and Switzerland that eased the burden.

Kohn: So you all think we should have concentrated on one target system if we could have?

LeMay: Just think what would have happened if we had taken the sorties that the heavies put on preparation for the invasion and suppression of the V–ls and the V–2s, and that sort of stuff, and laid them on the basic industry of Germany.[38]

Johnson: Of course, Spaatz, as I understand it, was told by Eisenhower that his mission was to get ashore in France and he had authority to use whatever force was necessary to do it. You can't blame Eisenhower for using every means at his disposal.

World War II: The Pacific

Kohn: It was different, however, in the Pacific where you were an

---

[38] In the winter and spring months of 1943–44, the Allied air forces had three major objectives: carrying the war directly to Germany through the Combined Bomber Offensive; conducting a sustained air interdiction campaign against German/French transportation and communication networks prior to the June 6, 1944, Normandy invasion; and, destroying the German rocket launching sites in northwest France from which the V–1 and V–2 rockets were being sent against Great Britain. In December 1943, the V–1 and V–2 rocket threat seemed to be the most ominous as British intelligence identified 75 sites in operation or under construction along the French coast. When the British Chiefs of Staff requested in December that Eighth Air Force's heavy bombers hit the rocket sites, the command complied while it continued to fly the Combined Bomber Offensive against Germany. Lt. Gen. Carl "Tooey" Spaatz, Commander, U.S. Strategic Air Forces, directed both bombing campaigns. From December to April, the number of Eighth Air Force sorties devoted to the rocket site attacks, called Operation CROSSBOW, escalated dramatically, reaching a peak of 4,150 in April 1944. In late March, General Eisenhower, who was Supreme Commander, Allied Expeditionary Forces, and Spaatz' immediate superior, adopted a British-conceived air interdiction plan (the Transportation Plan), which stipulated the use of virtually all of the Allied air forces against the transportation networks in western and northern France prior to the Normandy invasion. Spaatz complied, but the situation of multiple objectives and finite strategic air resources was creating strains within American and Allied commands. See Walt W. Rostow, *Pre-Invasion Bombing Strategy: General Eisenhower's Decision of 25 March 1944* (Austin, Tex., 1984); Haywood S. Hansell, Jr., *The Air Plan That Defeated Hitler* (Atlanta, 1972); Solly Zuckerman, *From Apes to Warlords: The Autobiography (1904–1946) of Solly Zuckerman* (New York, 1978); and Winston S. Churchill, *History of the Second World War*, vol 6, *Closing the Ring* (Boston, 1951).

independent command reporting directly to the JCS and you could choose the targets.[39]

LeMay: That's right. We weren't completely independent, however; we were taken off the strategic mission and put under Admiral Nimitz for the Okinawa invasion.[40]

Johnson: Oh, that's right.

Catton: The whole month of May 1945, the full month of May when the weather was superb, all we did was beat up the airfields on Kyūshū.

LeMay: I couldn't quarrel with the basic premise of stopping and helping the doughboys get ashore onto Okinawa. Our mission was to knock out the airfields on Kyūshū because the Navy was suffering the kamikaze attacks. But I did not think these attacks were too bad. The Navy only lost forty or

---

[39] Normally in World War II, commanders of operational forces—air, sea, or land—reported to the commanding general or admiral in a geographically designated "theater." In World War II in the Pacific, however, there were two theater commanders: General Douglas MacArthur in the Southwest Pacific Area, and Admiral Chester Nimitz in the Pacific Ocean Area. Both men reported directly to the U.S. Joint Chiefs of Staff. In 1944, the Army Air Forces activated for duty in the Pacific the Twentieth Air Force, which was an exception to the standard "theater" policy. This air force had two subordinate commands, the XX and XXI Bomber Commands, which contained all of the AAF's B-29 combat forces. These subordinate bomber commands were to be based in the Pacific—in China and the Mariana Islands—but they reported directly to Headquarters, Twentieth Air Force, located in Washington D.C. General Arnold served as commander of the Twentieth Air Force, and he reported directly to the Joint Chiefs of Staff on operational matters. The reason for this unusual arrangement was that Arnold wanted to keep direct control of the B-29s, believing that if they came under the control of one of the theater commanders the bombers would be directed away from a strategic campaign against Japan and used instead to support land and naval forces in the approach to the Japanese home islands. Although senior Navy leaders protested, the matter was settled in a joint Army-Navy conference in February 1944, with President Roosevelt concurring later. See Craven and Cate, *AAF in WWII*, IV, 36–37; Hansell, *The Strategic Air War Against Germany and Japan*, 157–160; Ronald H. Spector, *Eagle Against the Sun* (New York, 1984), 489–494; Grace P. Hayes, *The History of the Joint Chiefs of Staff in World War II: The War Against Japan* (Washington, 1982), 590–596.

[40] Fleet Adm. Chester W. Nimitz (1885–1966) graduated from the U.S. Naval Academy (1905) and became a submariner before World War I. An expert in submarine warfare and commander of a submarine division at age 26, Nimitz rose rapidly in rank and responsibility in the interwar Navy. By 1940 he was Chief of the Bureau of Navigation and following the Japanese attack on Pearl Harbor in December 1941, he was made CINCPACFLT (Commander-in-Chief, Pacific Fleet) and commander of all land, sea, and air forces in the Pacific Ocean Area. Headquartered in Honolulu, Hawaii, Admiral Nimitz directed the war against the Japanese in the northern and central Pacific Ocean areas. Admiral Nimitz, as theater commander, marshalled all theater forces for the Okinawa invasion. After the war Nimitz became the Chief of Naval Operations (1945–47).

fifty ships or something like that. Destroyers were the biggest ships sunk.[41]

Burchinal: They had some carrier damage.

LeMay: They had a few casualties, yes, but God, we were getting casualties every day.

Burchinal: You remember one admiral said, "Twenty-four more hours of

Maj. Jack Catton (left) and Gen. Haywood S. Hansell on the occasion of the arrival on Saipan of the first B–29. Courtesy Jack J. Catton

---

[41] On April 1, 1945, the Allies invaded the Japanese island of Okinawa. A massive naval flotilla of 1,200 ships, including more than 40 aircraft carriers, 18 battleships, and nearly 200 destroyers, carried more than 380,000 Marines and Army soldiers to the well-defended Japanese island. The Japanese defenders, anticipating the invasion, had devised superb defensive fortifications, including long-range artillery hidden in caves, machineguns placed at angles to produce withering crossfire patterns, and long-range artillery placements for use against American amphibious and naval forces. The Japanese also had assembled some 700 combat aircraft, half of them kamikaze suicide planes. During the invasion, the Japanese attacked the Allied flotilla assembled offshore. For eleven weeks the battle raged. For the men who remained shipboard the experience was one of seemingly endless alerts, suicidal enemy air attacks, artillery barrages from the hills, and large losses of men and machines. In all, the U.S. Navy had 4,900 sailors killed and 4,800 wounded. The U.S. Army and Marines lost 7,163 men, including the commanding general of the ground forces, Lt. Gen. Simon B. Bruckner, U.S. Army. The Japanese lost 70,000 military, 80,000 civilians, and the island. See Spector, *Eagle Against the Sun*, 532–540; Roy E. Appleman, James M. Burns, *et al.*, *Okinawa: The Last Battle*, vol 1, in *U.S. Army in World War II: The War in the Pacific* (Washington, 1948); Benis M. Frank and Henry I. Shaw, Jr., *Victory and Occupation*, vol 5, in *History of U.S. Marine Corps Operations in World War II* (Washington, 1968), 31–396; and Samuel Eliot Morison, *Victory in the Pacific*, vol 14, in *History of the United States Naval Operations in World War II* (Boston, 1960), 79–275.

this, and I quit." He threatened to pull out of the Okinawa operation because of the kamikazes. That was why we had to attack the airfields on a daily basis.

LeMay: The Navy actually sent a wire threatening to pull out if we stopped bombing Kyūshū. With that good weather, within a week, we had every airdrome completely flat, all of the facilities out. We didn't get all the airplanes because they would pull them off the fields, run them down the roads, and hide them under trees to save them for use as kamikazes. We postholed the fields, but we just couldn't stop a couple or three airplanes a day getting off the field. They would run a bunch of people out with baskets and fill up some holes and get the planes off with a half tank of gas. We couldn't stop that. When we were done, I went down to Nimitz and said, "Look, we have done everything that we can do. Turn us loose so we can go back to our primary mission." He put his arm around my shoulders and said, "Yes, you have done a fine job. I agree with you, but let's check with Sherman and see what he says." Sherman was the operations officer.[42] He not

Maj. Gen. Curtis LeMay (left) and Brig. Gen. Roger Ramey, Commander of the XX Bomber Command, pictured before LeMay's departure to assume command of the XXI Bomber Command.

---

[42] Adm. Forrest P. Sherman (1896–1951) graduated from the U.S. Naval Academy in 1917 and became a naval aviator in the 1920s. In the interwar years he remained in naval aviation, becoming in 1940 the fleet aviation officer for the United States Fleet, based in Norfolk, Virginia. In September 1942, Captain Sherman was commanding the *Wasp*, an aircraft carrier in the Pacific, when it sank under Japanese attack during the Battle of Guadalcanal. Subsequently, Sherman went to Honolulu and worked at Headquarters, U.S. Navy, Pacific Ocean Areas. During the battle for Okinawa in April 1945, Rear Admiral Sherman was Admiral Chester Nimitz's Deputy Chief of Staff for Plans.

only said, "No," he said, "Hell, no!" We ought to keep on. We spent another three weeks just postholing the fields. There was nothing left to bomb. We used up all of our delayed action fuses to confuse the issue a little bit and dropped bombs in there that would go off sometime later.

Kohn: That was only one month of the campaign.

Catton: One month, but how long was the campaign? You are dealing in very short periods of time now. Our real effort virtually began in 1945. Europe was over; we were now concentrating on Japan. Hell, one month out of that campaign was a very large percentage of the campaign.

LeMay: Remember, we just had a few months until the first of November when the invasion of the Japanese home islands was scheduled to begin.[43]

Burchinal: I remember at one point on Okinawa the Japanese had dug themselves into those cliffs way back in the caves. We were dropping napalm on them from B–29s at low level; then we figured out we had to drop the napalm inert and come in with firebombs to light it after it had dropped and seeped into the caves. To make it effective, we had to get the fire down into the caves. Talk about close air support!

Catton: It tells you something about the value and the versatility of long-range air; it really does. In many cases it is the only force you can apply.

LeMay: We got pulled off on other occasions. For example, I once got a message from the Joint Chiefs of Staff saying, "Support Halsey and his *soiree* against the Empire." His plan was to take the world's mightiest fleet and sail up to Japan. Starting down south, he would make a run in during the night, launch his airplanes, and then come back out, sail up the coast and go in

---

[43] In June 1945 when organized resistance ended on Okinawa, American military leaders reviewed final plans for the invasion of Japan. On June 18, 1945, the Joint Chiefs of Staff met with President Truman and outlined the plan for invading Kyūshū, the southernmost of the Japanese home islands. The JCS told the President the invasion would require 767,000 men and would probably, based on the Okinawa battle experience, result in 268,000 casualties. Some military intelligence experts predicted even greater losses. President Truman approved the Kyūshū invasion (Operation OLYMPIC) for November 1, 1945, and the invasion of Honshū (Operation CORONET), the next major island, for the spring of 1946. See Ray S. Cline, *Washington Command Post: The Operations Division*, in *U.S. Army in World War II: The War Department* (Washington, 1951), 333-362; Christopher Thorne, *Allies of a Kind: The United States, Britain, and the War Against Japan, 1941–1945* (New York, 1978), 520–525; James L. Stokesbury, *A Short History of World War II* (New York, 1980), 372–376.

again. If the weather was good and he ran two missions a day, he could drop 300 tons of bombs. That was his effort.[44]

I didn't volunteer anything. I just sat and waited for Halsey to tell me what he would like to have. Well, the fleet sailed from Ulithi, and I didn't hear anything. I was waiting for my naval liaison officer to tell me what they wanted, but nothing happened. Finally, after they sailed, I got a message from Halsey saying that he wanted me to support him with a maximum effort of the B–29 force against the airfields in the vicinity of his strikes. Now what was he asking for? Our maximum effort at that time was 3,000 tons. He was asking for 3,000 tons on airfields that weren't bothering anybody. We were sending reconnaissance airplanes and weather airplanes up there singlehanded, flying all over the place, and nobody bothered us. The Japanese were saving what airplanes they had left for use as kamikazes against the invasion. We weren't being attacked, so I sent a message to Halsey saying that I didn't think attacking airfields met the strategic mission. I suggested that I support him by hitting strategic targets in the area of his strikes. No message came back from Halsey. I got a message from Arnold that said, "Support Halsey in any way he asks."

I know what happened. Halsey had wired Nimitz, and Nimitz had wired King that I wasn't supporting Halsey.[45] Arnold said, "Oh, hell," and finally said, "Do it." I still wasn't licked, so I sent a message to Halsey that, okay, I would support him and hit the airfields—but to hit airfields, I had to have visual bombing conditions. The airfields didn't show up on the radar scopes, so I would have to have visual bombing conditions. If the weather was visual, I would hit those airdromes. If the weather was not visual, I would support him by hitting strategic targets in the area.

We had bad weather. He never got any air attacks from us.

---

[44] On July 1, 1945, the final naval campaign against Japan began. Adm. William F. Halsey and the Third Fleet sailed from Leyte Gulf in the Philippines with the objective of attacking the enemy's home islands, destroying the remnants of Japan's navy, merchant marine, and air forces, and crippling the nation's industrial and communications networks. Starting on July 10th, Halsey's Third Fleet sailed up and down the length of Japan, attacking at will. At this time General LeMay was commanding the XXI Bomber Command and was sending out as many as 500 B–29s, day and night, against Japanese cities and factories. Opposition was minimal. See Morison, *Victory in the Pacific 1945*, 298–336; Craven and Cate, *AAF in WWII*, V, 654–655.

[45] At this time the chain of command in the Central Pacific Theater ran upward from Fleet Admiral William F. Halsey, Commander of the Third Fleet, to Admiral Chester W. Nimitz, Commander, Pacific Ocean Areas, to Admiral Ernest King, Chief of Naval Operations and Commander-in-Chief, U.S. Fleet. As noted earlier, Maj. Gen. LeMay's command chain was different; he reported to General Arnold who was both the Commander of Twentieth Air Force and Commanding General, Army Air Forces. General George C. Marshall was the Chief of Staff, U.S. Army. The three ranking officers for sea, air, and land forces—Admiral King, General Arnold, and General Marshall—together with President Roosevelt's personal representative, Admiral William D. Leahy, constituted the United States' Joint Chiefs of Staff during the war.

Kohn: What was different when you got over to the Pacific? How was it different from the European environment? Did you talk about that down in the wings? You had not been in Europe, General Catton.

Catton: I was not in Europe, no.

Kohn: General Burchinal, you were in Europe.

Burchinal: I was over there in late 1942, but I was not on the bombing side.

LeMay: The main difference, I think, was that we could fool the Japanese once in a while with diversions and such, but we never fooled the Germans. I think the Germans had a better radar net and a better defense setup, and we had virtually trained them for a period of time with our piddling raids early in the war. The Japanese didn't have that training. I remember "Monty" Montgomery, my ops officer, telling me this story (he went with the Strategic Bombing Survey into Japan after the war).[46]

The Survey team went into the central fighter control setup there, and Monty asked the question, "What happens here now when the radar sees the B–29s coming?" The answer was, "All lights light; all bells ring."[47]

Kohn: Did you change any of your methods?

Burchinal: There were two different parts to the campaign. The first were the early missions from the China-Burma-India theater. Then there were the early ones from the Marianas. From the Marianas we didn't do things very

---

[46] Maj. Gen. John B. Montgomery (1911–87) was commissioned in the Army Air Corps in February 1936. A bomber pilot prior to the war, he became an operational planner when the war began. Working at Headquarters, Army Air Forces, Montgomery assisted in planning the strategic bombing campaign in Europe as a staff officer in the Office of the Chief of Bombardment. Late in 1944, he went to the Marianas with the XXI Bomber Command. That command was one of the two bomber commands of the Twentieth Air Force, the AAF's long-range strategic air force in the Pacific. In November 1944, Colonel Montgomery became the Deputy Chief of Staff for Operations for the bomber command. When General LeMay assumed command in January 1945, he served on his headquarters staff for the balance of the war. From 1948 to 1955, a period when LeMay was building the Strategic Air Command, General Montgomery was the command's Deputy Chief of Staff for Operations, and then Eighth Air Force Commander.

[47] The U.S. Strategic Bombing Survey was established by President Franklin D. Roosevelt in the fall of 1944 to measure the effectiveness of strategic bombing in the Allied victory. Fourteen hundred officers, enlisted personnel, and civilians constituted the European survey team, and another 1,100 made up the team surveying the Pacific theater. The Survey's lasting record is impressive: (1) a definitive record of the strategic bombing effort; (2) a lengthy series of reports, each carefully researched and checked against available enemy records; (3) a series of conclusions comparing prewar strategic air doctrine with wartime performance. For a history of the Survey and its findings, see David MacIsaac, *Strategic Bombing in World War Two: The Story of the United States Strategic Bombing Survey* (New York, 1976).

well at the beginning because we used the B–29 as a very high-altitude airplane. We put it up at 32,000 feet; the Japanese fighters would hang on their props trying to get up there. But we also ran into jetstreams of 180 and 200 knots, and we had never run into those before.[48]

Catton: I led our group on the first mission out of the Marianas, it was an entirely different situation than the raids run out of India through China. We flew in formation all the way from Saipan staying low to the start-climb point for the purpose of saving fuel. We were still carrying a bomb-bay tank then, as you will recall. Then we climbed to put ourselves at altitude before we made landfall, which was very telling on the airplanes. So our altitude on the first mission was 35,000 feet.

Burchinal: If you could get there.

Catton: As we were approaching the Island of Honshū, I had never seen drift like we were experiencing. We were heading north, and we were encountering for the first time the jetstream. The correction that we had to make to hit the IP [initial point] was something like 20 degrees. At any rate, turning over the IP we suddenly found ourselves far downwind. We had a bunch of clouds, not total cover, but a bunch of clouds, and I have to tell you that the speed on the bomb run was very, very much to our disadvantage in acquiring sighting and getting the bombs on the target.

Burchinal: The bombsight couldn't handle it. It would spin, and it couldn't handle that speed.

Kohn: Was it the same bombsight in the B–29 as on the B–17, General Burchinal?

Catton: Yes, we had a Norden bombsight.

LeMay: The winds were so high that if you bombed crosswind to the jetstream the bombsight wouldn't take the drift that you needed; it was too great.

---

[48] Strategic air operations in the Pacific began in June 1944 and ended in August 1945. Initially, the B–29s flew from bases in China and used precision bombing tactics in attacking iron and steel factories in Manchuria and Japan. Then in late November 1944, B–29 operations began from bases in the Mariana Islands in the Central Pacific. These Marianas bombing operations also used bombing tactics developed in Europe where Eighth and Fifteenth Air Force B–17s and B–24s were attacking specific military and industrial targets. In January 1945 the Joint Chiefs of Staff, acting on the advice of General Arnold, shut down the strategic air operations in China and transferred the B–29s of the XX Bomber Command to the Marianas. See Craven and Cate, *AAF in WWII*, V, 92–179, 608–676.

Catton: So you either had to go upwind or downwind to hold down the drift.

Burchinal: If you went upwind . . .

LeMay: You sat there forever.

Burchinal: You would be there until you ran out of fuel.

LeMay: If you came downwind then the bombardier had a hard time getting synchronized.

Burchinal: You were doing 500 to 525 knots.

Catton: We had a tough time there for the first several months of operations out of the Marianas learning the use of the airplane at those altitudes. It was the combination of materiel problems—particularly the engines—and the difficulty with the jetstream. So we were not very successful. We gradually made changes to accommodate those problems.

LeMay: When I got to India, fresh out of Europe, our force didn't have standard tactics.[49] They had gone on some missions at night and some in daytime, individually, and in formation, but nothing much standard.

Every time you would fly a mission out of China to Japan, you encountered weather—the weather was worse there than it was in Europe. During the best month of the year there was an average of only seven days that would permit visual bombing from altitude; the worst month of the year, there was only one day. We had to forecast that day and be up there over the target; we didn't get any weather reports out of Japan, of course, and the Russians wouldn't give us any. There was one Navy station up in the Gobi Desert. (Why the Navy was up there, I never did find out, but they were there.) Once in a while they would send out a weather report. I established a station at Mao Zedong's headquarters in northern China. I sent a radio set and a team of officers up there, including a weatherman. The Japanese controlled all of the main cities, the railroads, the roads, and the lines of communications, but there were large areas of China, particularly in the south, that Chiang's troops controlled. There were big areas in the north that Mao Zedong controlled. If we had an airplane go down in one of Chiang's

---

[49] India was the location for five large Army Air Forces staging bases for the B–29s flying out of China. Constructed in early 1944, these bases were used as training bases, logistical depots, and staging sites for operations. The advanced base in China was at Chengtu. There were two problems in operating from India: first, there was little or no aviation fuel in China; second, the fuel for the B–29s had to be airlifted from India across the Himalaya Mountains to China. It took ten gallons of aviation gas to deliver one gallon "over the hump" to the B–29 forces in China. See William H. Tunner, *Over the Hump* (New York, 1964; reprint, Washington, 1985), 129–135; Craven and Cate, *AAF in WWII*, IV, 405–548, V, 179–200.

Above: **Tons of bombs are being loaded on the B–29 Superfortress before delivery to Japanese war production centers;** *below*: **B–29 in flight.**

areas, we would get word by radio where it was, and we could send help. Not so in Mao's areas. The two were bitter enemies.[50]

Saying nothing, I sent my men up to Mao, knowing how they would be received. They asked him if he would let us know if an airplane went down in his area so we could send help. Mao not only said "yes" but he offered to build us airdromes in his area. Well, since we couldn't supply the fields we had in the south, I recommended only that he improve his field at his headquarters. I would set up a radio station and supply it if he would notify me about downed aircraft and help our people out. Well, he agreed, and we would get radio reports from there.

However, we had nothing on which to draw maps. The only way we could draw a weather map was send some B–29s up to see what the weather looked like, and try to draw maps from that, then make forecasts of how to set up a mission. On top of that, when ordered to fly a mission out of China, we had to make seven trips with a B–29 and offload all the gas we could, leaving only enough to get back to India. On the eighth trip we would transport a load of bombs, top off with gas in China, and go drop them on Japan if the weather was right. Then we'd start the process all over again. So the logistical situation was hopeless in China. We didn't get much accomplished. We ran some decent missions; I think we stopped the main Japanese drive in China in 1944 by bombing Hankow, their main supply base, and on that mission did a little experimental work with the incendiaries.[51] We knocked out Formosa pretty well before the Okinawa show, but we really didn't get much done.

---

[50] Mao Zedong (1893–1976) and Chiang Kai-shek (1887–1975) led the two rival forces struggling for control of China in the twentieth century. The rivalry began in the 1920s when the revolutionary movement of Dr. Sun Yat-Sen split into two factions. Mao was the principal Chinese marxist theorist, soldier, and leader in the struggle against Chiang Kai-shek's Nationalist Chinese government. Chiang Kai-shek was a general and leader of the Chinese Nationalist government from 1928 to 1949, and subsequently, the Nationalist government in exile on Taiwan from 1949 to 1975. For almost thirty years, 1920 to 1949, the Nationalists and the Communists fought for control of China. In 1931 Japan seized Manchuria, China's northern province, and in 1937 the Japanese invaded central China and forced Chaing's government and armies to retreat into the interior provinces in the south. Mao's Communist armies, enlarged and restructured to face the Japanese threat, were located in the northern provinces. See Jerome Ch'en, *Mao and the Chinese Revolution* (London, 1965); Maurice Meisner, *Mao's China: A History of the Peoples Republic* (New York, 1977); Barbara W. Tuchman, *Stilwell and the American Experience in China* (New York, 1970).

[51] Hankow, China, was a Japanese-controlled city in central China. Japanese forces were using it as a supply base for a major offensive into southern China in late 1944. On December 8, 1944, General LeMay sent 94 B–29s over Hankow where they dropped incendiary bombs. Although smoke and debris obliterated the target areas for most of the B–29s, damage to the city was severe: 40–50 percent burned out. Maj. Gen. Claire Chennault, Commander of Fourteenth Air Force and Air Advisor to General Chiang Kai-shek, said that the raid "destroyed Hankow as a major base." Craven and Cate, *AAF in WWII*, V, 143–144.

Kohn: So you moved the B–29 force to the Marianas.[52]

LeMay: When the Marianas opened up, the decision was made to move out there. I didn't make that decision; it was made back in Washington. In my reports I recommended no more B–29s be sent to India because they weren't getting as much done.

Kohn: It was in the Marianas that you changed tactics . . .

LeMay: I got over to the Marianas in January 1945. We started off with the standard tactics that had proved successful in Europe. Here again: weather. After we readied the crews, loaded the bombs, and gassed the aircraft, we would sit and wait on the weather. I woke up at the end of about six weeks and realized that we hadn't got much done; the invasion of Japan was scheduled for the end of the year. "Stan" Emrick, my chief of maintenance, was doing a lot of thinking and planning over there, and he came in and told me one day, thinking about the invasion, that because we had changed our maintenance system, we were capable of flying every airplane and every air crew an average of 120 hours a month.[53] We only had to hoop up the supply level a little bit. So I told Nimitz about that, but got the back of the hand: "You can't do this; you only flew 30 hours a month over in England where you had all this industrial support around you; out in the boondocks, how are you going to fly 120?" I said, "Well, we have a new maintenance system and a different setup; we can do it." We never got to first base with the Navy. I finally got mad and said, "Tell them down there that we are going to do it, and if we run out of supplies, they can tell the Joint Chiefs of Staff: We will go fishing." We ran out of incendiary bombs, remember, at the end of the five missions when we started the low-altitude stuff, and we didn't have another one then for about 6 weeks, except, I guess, for one small raid with a few bombs.

---

[52] The B–29s stationed in India and China were relocated to Tinian and Guam Islands in the Marianas in the early spring of 1945 where they joined the B–29 forces already based there. The War Department order was issued on February 6, 1945. A few weeks prior, on January 18th, LeMay had been transferred to the Marianas to command the XXI Bomber Command, Twentieth Air Force.

[53] Lt. Gen. Paul Stanley Emrick, (1914–) graduated from Purdue University (1938) with a degree in mechanical engineering. He joined the Army Air Corps in 1939, becoming a fighter pilot. In World War II, Emrick served successively in the United States in bomber units, first in training, then in planning. In June 1944 he went to China, joining the B–29 units of the Twentieth Air Force. When General LeMay left China for the Marianas, Colonel Emrick accompanied him, becoming in a few weeks the chief maintenance officer for the XXI Bomber Command. He served with LeMay for the duration of the war. In the postwar Air Force, Emrick also worked with General LeMay in 1946–47 in developing requirements for the B–52 long-range bomber. Later in the 1950s Emrick served as the Strategic Air Command's Inspector General and Director of Plans.

Kohn: You stood down for six weeks for the lack of incendiary bombs?

Burchinal: Well, we kept on with daylight bombing using high explosive bombs.

LeMay: In six weeks the Navy found some ships and we got incendiary bombs again, but we never caught up from then until the end of the war. We would persuade the Marines, who, were supposed to be resting to get up at four o'clock in the morning and haul bombs for us until breakfast time. Then they would go off on their mission, or we would get the Seabees to do it. We hauled bombs from the ships to the hardstands and skipped the bomb dumps from then on until the end of the war.

Our whole goal was to try to end the war before the invasion. We were not going to be able to do it continuing on like we were, given the weather and the problem of high-altitude visual bombing. We just didn't have enough airplanes and enough time. So we had to do something radical. We had always been thinking about incendiary attacks against the vulnerable Japanese cities. All the figures indicated we had to have at least 400 airplanes to get enough concentration to start really large fires, and we didn't have 400 airplanes.

We also started looking at radar bombing. In England before I left, we had gotten some of the early radars over in a few airplanes. We didn't get any good out of it at all. They couldn't even find Frankfurt, a big city in the middle of Germany. We sent the radar-equipped planes as lead aircraft on a mission against Frankfurt, planning if we couldn't see the main target to drop by radar. It did not work well. The APQ–13 was supposed to be better, but how much better I did not know.[54] We had a professor from Massachusetts Institute of Technology out there who had been in the radar program right from the start. So I sent him up to "Rosie" O'Donnell's outfit on Saipan and told him to fly with about a dozen of the stupidest radar operators he could find and see if they could fly over this spit of land sticking out of the northern

---

[54] Two basic radars were used in World War II: AN/APQ–13 and AN/APQ–7. The former was developed in the war as a navigational aid. It consisted of a radar mounted on the aircraft and two or more fixed beacons on land or sea. The aircraft radar operator or navigator queried the beacons and by triangulation located the aircraft at a fixed point. Once the aircraft's position was known, the navigator could plan a route to the other known position: the target. In early bombing operations over Europe, the AN/APQ–13 radar was inaccurate and unreliable. The AN/APQ–7 radar was a product of the war, developed at the MIT Lincoln Laboratories specifically for long-range bombing. It was mounted on the aircraft, but with an electromagnetic scanner which allowed a significantly higher degree of resolution. The aircraft's radar scanned the horizon for prepositioned beacons. Once located or fixed, the radar gave the navigator accurate data on the location of the bomber. Using maps of the target area, the navigator took the information from the radar system and calculated the course to the target. See Arthur Roberts, ed., *Radar Beacons* (New York, 1947), 14–17.

part of Saipan.[55] He came back shaking his head; he just could not understand how poorly trained the operators were. But he said, yes, he thought most of them could do that. Our first attack on Tokyo was just that; it was a little spit of land sticking out below Tokyo in the Tokyo Bay. Our people flew over it, turned to a compass heading to which they were assigned, flew for so many seconds, then pulled the string. That was our start.

I also started a radar school to train our people better. As we got better people, we put them up in front of the formations. On the first attack I had our better people out front to start with, but as our people became trained and achieved proficiency, we actually destroyed an industrial area on an inland town in the middle of a thunderstorm. With training, radar became an important aid. Thus if you could get your airplanes ready, loaded with bombs, and the crews ready to go, gas and everything, and if the weather was good, we would hit one of the high-priority visual targets that we were assigned. If the weather was bad, which it usually was, we did not sit and wait until it got better; we flew a low-altitude mission against an industrial area target. Eventually we did fly 120 hours a month. The reason we went to low altitude was that we didn't have 400 airplanes. So I took out the guns and the gunners, reducing the weight so we could increase the bomb load. I think the first mission we ran against Tokyo was about 350 airplanes. It was enough; it was highly successful.[56]

Kohn: Did you know what the effects would be? Did you think incendiaries would, in effect . . .

Burchinal: Back on 25 February, the first time we had a 200-ship raid, over

---

[55] Gen. Emmett ("Rosie") O'Donnell, (1905–72) was a native of Brooklyn, New York. A graduate of the U.S. Military Academy (1928), he joined the Army Air Corps, becoming a fighter pilot. He flew in pursuit groups for six years before returning to West Point to coach football. In 1938, O'Donnell retrained into bombers and was in the Philippines in December 1941 when the war began. When the Japanese attacked, he managed to get his B–17 aloft and attacked a Japanese cruiser and destroyer escort. Early in the war he served in the Philippines (1941–42), Java (1942), India (1942), and the United States (1943), at one point serving on General Arnold's Advisory Council. In February 1944 he became Commanding General, 73d Bomb Wing, one of the first B–29 wings sent to the Pacific Theater. In late 1944–45 he led the wing in a series of strikes against Japan. When General LeMay assumed command in January 1945, O'Donnell continued to command the wing until Japan's surrender in September 1945. In the postwar years, O'Donnell led combat air forces in the Strategic Air Command and the Far East Air Forces during the Korean War. Finally, he served as the Commanding General, Pacific Air Forces, from 1959 to 1963.

[56] On February 25, 1945, LeMay sent 231 B–29s to bomb Tokyo in the largest strategic strike of the Pacific war to that date. Each B–29 bomber carried one 500-pound general purpose bomb and numerous E-46 incendiary bombs. In all, 172 B–29s reached Tokyo, dropping 453.7 tons of bombs. The results, like the size of the effort, exceeded all previous air strikes. According to the records of the Tokyo police, 27,970 buildings were destroyed in the raid. See Craven and Cate, *AAF in WWII*, V, 572–573; Schaffer, *Wings of Judgment*, 124–128.

Effect of strategic bombing by B–29s on a section of Tokyo.

200, we went against Tokyo at high altitude. In the bomb load were some incendiaries. It was a total radar attack; the weather was lousy. But from photo reconnaissance after the mission, we realized we had burned out a pretty respectable chunk of Kawasaki, the first area we hit.[57] So we knew the effect was there; Japan would burn if we could get fire on it.

Kohn: Had you discussed at all the idea, before February, of altering the whole character of the campaign? Or, was it a matter of seeing what happened and saying, "Gee, this might work?"

Catton: Let me add a little bit to what General LeMay is saying, but from a little bit different perspective. When he arrived from India to take command of the then XXI Bomber Command, which eventually became Twentieth Air Force down at Harmon Field, Guam, I had a lead crew, and I was about to get a squadron. We had achieved some successes in January and early

---

[57] Kawasaki, a populous industrial suburb of 300,000, was located immediately south of Tokyo and north of Yokohama, the large port city for Tokyo.

February, for example, doing a lot better than we described originally. When General LeMay arrived, from a crew point of view, there was a very substantial change. The training, the development, and the selection of lead crews became very prominent, much more so than it had been in the past. For at least a week (I don't recall now—you will, Dave), for a week or two, we didn't fly combat; we flew training missions around the Marianas. General LeMay was airborne during those training exercises. We practiced formation flying. We were practicing for day visual bombing at appropriate altitudes, and at altitudes where we would have substantial fighter opposition. We *trained*; I will never forget that. We flew nearly every other day on training missions, and I can remember the boss sitting up there saying things like, "Okay, lead of the 498th, if you can't do a better job of lead, then change lead—now." We really were in a training environment. We all got the message very, very clearly and learned that the leadership of the formation, just as General Johnson was saying, had to be far better than it had been in the past. So formation leads then became a very important criterion in terms of crew, aircraft, equipment, tactics, techniques—the tactical doctrine was refined. We really improved in doctrine and training. That's when General LeMay opened up the lead crew school at Muroc, as I recall. About that time we also began to make use of the APQ–7 radar and achieved the versatility to make the application of the force effective. I do want to underline the fact that we had achieved some success before General LeMay got there, but after General LeMay arrived, we really put our nose to the stone in terms of training, doctrine, and *air discipline*. It really paid off for the daylight visual missions.

LeMay: That was early when we were still following the European pattern. At that rate we could get missions off doing high-altitude bombing, but the weather wasn't going to let us do the job; we weren't going to finish the job before the invasion. So we had to do something radical.

Kohn: You were focusing on that point; you were trying to defeat Japan specifically by means of strategic air power, and there were no ifs, ands, or buts about it.

LeMay: That's right.

Catton: The point I am making is that even though we didn't have the force size required to do it with day visual bombing, we were good at day visual bombing in that springtime. We were doing a good job under the circumstances.

LeMay: If you could get the weather to do it.

Catton: Right. Exactly.

Burchinal: Didn't you make a trip back here then to talk to Arnold about holding off the land invasion?[58]

LeMay: No.

Burchinal: Or did you send it through by message? Because we got turned down. Arnold did go to Marshall, but then he backed him when Marshall said, "We are going to have an invasion."[59] This was perhaps in May 1945.

LeMay: General Arnold came out to visit us. Remember when he came?

Burchinal: That's right. He came to visit us.[60]

---

[58] Gen. Henry H. "Hap" Arnold (1886–1950). Following graduation from West Point (1908), Arnold decided on a career in military aviation. He learned to fly from the Wright brothers in 1911 and set numerous military aeronautical records. During World War I he served on the War Department General Staff in Washington. In the 1920s and 1930s Arnold remained in the small Army Air Service and Air Corps, rising in rank and holding several significant commands. In September 1938, he became Chief of the Air Corps, with the rank of major general. During World War II, General Arnold served as Commanding General, Army Air Forces (AAF). The AAF expanded during his tenure from 22,000 airmen and 3,900 aircraft to 2,400,000 men and women and 75,000 airplanes. During the war, General Arnold suffered several heart attacks, causing him to retire in 1946. He was succeeded by General Carl Spaatz. A recent biography is Thomas A. Coffey, *HAP: The Story of the U.S. Air Force and the Man Who Built It, General Henry H. "Hap" Arnold* (New York, 1982); see also John W. Huston, "The Wartime Leadership of 'Hap Arnold'," *Air Power and Warfare, Proceedings of the 8th Military History Symposium, USAF Academy, October 18–20, 1978*, eds. Alfred F. Hurley and Robert C. Ehrhart, (Washington, 1979), 168–185.

[59] Gen. George C. Marshall (1890–1959) was the Army Chief of Staff from 1939 to 1945. A brilliant strategist and statesman, Marshall has been credited with being the architect and organizer of the United States victory in World War II. He was one of the most significant American statesmen of the twentieth century. In May-June 1945, General Marshall and War Department planners were reviewing the final details of Operations OLYMPIC and CORONET, the Allied invasion of Kyūshū and Honshū, the two major islands constituting Japan. Air and naval leaders tried to make the case that military pressure, if air and sea operations continued uninterrupted, would become so great against Japan that it would surrender and the invasion would not be necessary. Marshall and his planners disagreed, citing the fanatical Japanese defense of Okinawa. Subsequently, all senior military leaders, including General Arnold and Admiral King, agreed on the plan to invade Japan. See Forrest C. Pogue, *George C. Marshall*, 4 vols, (New York, 1963–1987), vol 3, 582–583; Cline, *Washington Command Post*, 333–346.

[60] General Arnold flew to the Pacific on June 8, 1945, visiting the Marianas Islands and the B–29 forces June 12–17, 1945. He returned to the United States on June 25th. See Henry H. Arnold, *Global Mission* (New York, 1949), 561–575.

Maj. Jack Catton with his combat crew on Saipan. Catton is kneeling, 3rd from left. Courtesy Jack J. Catton

LeMay: And we gave him a briefing on what we had been doing, and what we were going to do. If he hadn't been convinced before, I think he was convinced then that we could do the job, because he asked me when the war was going to end. I said, "Well, we have been so busy fighting it I haven't figured out a date. We are trying to end it before the invasion. Give me thirty minutes, and I will give you a date." So I got Monty and "Jim" Garcia and Stan Emrick to take a look and see how many more industrial areas we had to hit and how long it was going to take us.[61] They came back in about twenty minutes, and we gave Arnold a date in September sometime. He said immediately: "You will go back to brief the Joint Chiefs."

Burchinal: That's when you left.

LeMay: Yes. I went back to Washington to brief the Joint Chiefs. Arnold wanted it done right away, and as a matter of fact, he forgot the international date line. We couldn't make the scheduled appointment with the JCS that he had made, so we delayed a day. We flew nonstop to Hawaii and then took off from Hawaii, but we could not get a clearance straight to Washington. We were only cleared through San Francisco. We tried to get a radio clearance from San Francisco, but we ran out of radio range before we could get it. We never were cleared. When we showed up at the Washington National Airport, they said, "We don't have any record of you. Where did you take off from?" I said, "Honolulu." They said, "Honolulu!"

---

[61] Colonels John B. Montgomery, James D. Garcia, and Stanley Emrick were, respectively, General LeMay's chief deputies for operations, intelligence, and plans for the XXI Bomber Command, Twentieth Air Force. For Montgomery and Emrick see previous notes. Colonel Garcia was a graduate of the U.S. Military Academy (1939) who entered the Army Air Corps in 1940. He rose from second lieutenant to colonel in less than four years.

We briefed the Joint Chiefs of Staff; of course Arnold wasn't there. We did not get a very good reception. As a matter of fact, General Marshall slept through most of the briefing. I can't blame him; he was probably worn down to a nub. The decision was made to invade. Here was a crazy flyboy coming in saying the war could be ended without invasion. We didn't make much of an imprint. So we went back to the Marianas and did it anyway.[62]

Burchinal: After that trip we made a change: from there on, we were going to fly max effort, logistically. We were going to burn the crews out. To hell with crew rotation, we were going to burn them out because we thought we could end the war. The crew replacement program wasn't going to provide crews fast enough to replace crews which would complete the number of missions required to return home. That's when the bombs came off the ships onto the hardstands and never got to the bomb dump. It was just max effort from there on out to knock the Japanese out of the war. Night and day.

Kohn: Did you feel under pressure from Washington, that General Arnold was trying to prove something about air power?

Burchinal: No. The pressure wasn't in Washington; it was right here [pointing to LeMay].

LeMay: I never felt that they were looking over my shoulder from Washington. That wasn't there; it was our own idea. I did the initial low-altitude attack on Tokyo without asking anybody. Norstad came out there once, and I tried to sound him out as to General Arnold's wishes.[63] I didn't

---

[62] LeMay's briefing to the Joint Chiefs of Staff on June 19, 1945, was one of several briefings on the issue of the invasion of Japan. Earlier in the spring of 1945, Army and Navy planners developed detailed plans for the invasion, and on May 25 the JCS sent these plans to Admiral Nimitz and General MacArthur, the respective Pacific theater commanders. Throughout June the Joint Chiefs held meetings with White House officials about the invasion. By the end of the month, a coordinated American invasion strategy had been approved by President Truman. It called for a massive amphibious invasion of Kyūshū, the southernmost of the main Japanese islands, by 767,000 troops in November 1945 (Operation OLYMPIC); followed by the invasion of Honshū, the largest of the Japanese islands, in March 1946 (Operation CORONET). Prior to these invasions, the combined strategic air assault and naval blockade would continue. See Cline, *Washington Command Post*, 340–380; Arnold, *Global Mission*, 564–567; Robert W. Coakley and Richard M. Leighton, *Global Logistics and Strategy 1943–1945* in *U.S. Army in World War II: The War Department* (Washington, 1968), 563–564, 578–588, 617–618.

[63] Maj. Gen. Norstad was General Arnold's Chief of Staff for the Twentieth Air Force. Arnold actually commanded this specialized air force from Washington, but because of his many obligations in leading the Army Air Forces and in serving on the Joint Chiefs of Staff, Norstad became his principal agent at Headquarters AAF in planning and overseeing the combat operations of the Twentieth in the Marianas. Schaffer, *Wings of Judgment*, 121–127, 128–142.

know Arnold very well. I had only met him once. Although he was commanding March Field when I was a flying cadet, I had never met him. I only met him on the way back from England to go to the Pacific.

Kohn: Did he give you any specific instructions then?

LeMay: No. And I never felt that they were looking over my shoulder. I knew what was expected of me and why I was there. I had to produce some results.

Kohn: Did you attempt to define those results, General LeMay? Did you have anything specific in mind?

LeMay: Once we successfully attacked Tokyo, it became apparent that if we trained the radar operators properly, then we could get the maximum hours and sorties out of our force, for use against the industrial areas. Then we would really get something done. That is what we were concentrating on.

I was still following my instructions from Washington on the priority of targets. If we were sure of the weather, we would do a visual attack on priority targets. If we weren't sure of the weather, we would go after the industrial areas.

Burchinal: Attacking at low altitude also let us put in ten tons, 20,000 pounds, of bombs in the bomb bay.

Catton: The airplanes operated magnificently. We carried a maximum load of bombs, our losses went way down, and our effectiveness went way up.

Participating in discussions following Germany's surrender, from left to right, are Maj. Gen. Lauris Norstad, Gen. Henry H. Arnold, and Gen. George C. Marshall.

Burchinal: In June 1945 we did another thing, also. By then there wasn't any fighter opposition. If you saw a fighter, it was incredible. Our doctrine had always been to hit a target and keep hitting it until it disappeared, until we had destroyed it. At that point we took a briefing to General LeMay. We said, "What we want to do now is damage—not destroy—the maximum number of targets. Put them out of action. We want to break the attack into squadron formations and give a target to a squadron instead of to a whole wing or a group."

General LeMay said, "OK." That greatly multiplied force effectiveness for short-term shock effect. Whenever we could fly day—visual—we had individual targets. The principal ground defenses, the AA fire, were centered around the big cities. The smaller areas, had little defense, but railyards and POL [petroleum, oil, and lubricants] targets and other meaningful targets were there to hit for squadron-size efforts.[64]

LeMay: By this time the lead crew business had started paying off, and we were getting some good visual bombing missions. I remember once betting "Butch" Blanchard ten bucks that we couldn't do as good a job on a certain Japanese steel mill as they did on the cement plant in India that we had used for practice runs.[65]

Finally we got a pattern of bombs on a target that was as good; I lost the $10, and Butch framed it. But actually there weren't enough visual days to do the overall job we wanted. Actually my target list came from the world almanac that we used for picking out the biggest industrial areas.

Catton: We owned the air, and the opposition was minimal, so you could spread the force without risk of high attrition.

---

[64] Within the Twentieth Air Force, the average squadron had 15 B–29s.

[65] Gen. William H. "Butch" Blanchard (1916–66). In the spring of 1945, Colonel Blanchard was General LeMay's Assistant Chief of Staff for Operations in the XXI Bomber Command. A West Point graduate (1939), Blanchard led the combat crew training section for the first B–29 unit formed in 1943. He piloted the first B–29 to China and subsequently was commanding officer of the 40th Bomb Group, XX Bomber Command in Chengtu, China, from August 1944 to January 1945. When that command moved its operations in early 1945 from China to the Marianas, Colonel Blanchard became LeMay's operations officer, helping plan and direct the low-level incendiary strikes and the atomic missions against Japan. In the postwar years General Blanchard held key command and staff positions in the Strategic Air Command (1946–60), serving as commanding officer of the 509th Bomb Wing (1946–48), the first atomic-capable wing in the Air Force. Subsequently, he was Director of Operations at Eighth Air Force (1948–52), Deputy Director of Operations at Headquarters SAC (1953–56), and Commander of SAC's Seventh Air Division (1957–60). In October 1961, Lt. Gen. Blanchard became Inspector General at Headquarters, USAF. He remained at that headquarters serving in the key deputates of programs and requirements, and plans and operations before becoming in February 1965 the Vice Chief of Staff of the Air Force. Four months later, he suffered a heart attack and died.

Burchinal: As long as you stayed out of the heavy AA areas, you were pretty much home free.

LeMay: In other words what we were trying to do was make maximum use of the tools we had, to get the maximum use out of them; tactics and everything went out the window.

Johnson: I have been quiet all this time because I wasn't involved in this, but I do think, going back to pressure, that General Arnold kept pressure on everyone to keep going and moving and moving. I talked to Larry Norstad for three hours recently at his home. Arnold put General LeMay there to put the pressure on because he knew General LeMay would do it. There wasn't any question about that; he wanted more bombs on those targets. He wanted them everywhere.

Burchinal: Earlier we were getting it from Arnold—before Curt showed up in the Pacific—because we weren't doing much then. The results were not very encouraging.

Johnson: Twining, who had the Fifteenth Air Force down in Italy in World War II, was bombing away, and he told a couple of us this story perhaps ten years ago.[66] The war was about to end in Europe, and Arnold came down to see him. Arnold said, "Nate, you are doing a lousy job down here. How are you going to get this war finished unless you get more bombs on those targets? Old "Joe" Cannon over there is doing a lousy job with the Twelfth.[67]

---

[66] Gen. Nathan F. Twining (1897–1982) was one of General Arnold's combat commanders in World War II. A professional soldier who graduated from the U.S. Military Academy in 1918, Twining had risen slowly to the rank of colonel in the Army Air Corps before the Japanese attack on Pearl Harbor. In the spring of 1942 Twining went to the South Pacific as a brigadier general, serving as Chief of Staff, Allied Air Forces and Commanding General, Thirteenth Air Force. In the Pacific he directed the tactical air operations in the Solomon Islands Campaign. In November 1943 he became Commander, Fifteenth Air Force, then based in Italy. This air force participated in the Combined Bomber Offensive against Germany throughout 1944-45. When Arnold visited him in May 1945, General Twining was commanding both Fifteenth Air Force and the Mediterranean Allied Strategic Air Forces. Following the war Twining held a variety of key commands, culminating in his selection as USAF Chief of Staff in June 1953. On March 26, 1957, President Eisenhower nominated Twining to be Chairman of the Joint Chiefs of Staff. He was the first Air Force officer to hold that position. He retired in September 1960.

[67] Gen. John K. Cannon (1892–1955) became associated with the development of tactical air forces early in World War II. A specialist in training pilots and devising air tactics before the war, Cannon led air units in support of the Allied invasions of North Africa, Sicily, and Italy. Late in 1943 he was given command of Twelfth Air Force and the Mediterranean Allied Tactical Air Command. As such, Cannon led the tactical air forces for General Mark Clark's Fifth Army in Italy. At the time of Arnold's visit to Twining in May, 1945, General Cannon was Commander of Twelfth Air Force and Commander-in-Chief, Allied Air Forces in the Mediterranean Theater. In the postwar years Cannon commanded the Air Training Command (1946–48), United States Air Forces, Europe (1948–50), and Tactical Air Command (1950–54).

We will be here forever if you all don't get to work and do a better job." Just at that time a sergeant came in and handed Nate a piece of paper. He looked at it. Arnold said, "What's that?" Twining handed it to Arnold and said, "The Germans have just unconditionally surrendered."

LeMay: There is a picture of that, isn't there?

Johnson: Arnold looked at the note and said, "Get me a camera." Tom Steed was there, and Tom said, "General, you don't need a camera; we have plenty of people." Arnold said, "Get me a camera." Tom insisted, "Why do you want a camera?" Arnold replied, "I want to photograph the fauna and the flora." Arnold was simply through with war. He was a driver. Through the years we have not realized how much we owe him, and how he drove that air force.[68]

LeMay: I knew what was expected of me out in the Pacific, but I didn't feel that I was being lashed by General Arnold back in the Pentagon.

Johnson: No one felt that Arnold was lashing, but he demanded and he expected it. I knew that.

Kohn: Did you all feel in the Pacific that you had done the job without the atomic bomb, that the atomic bomb was, in a sense, just icing on the cake?

LeMay: It wasn't exactly icing on the cake. It is true that the war was over before the atomic bomb was dropped. We knew that because we had broken their code; we knew the Japanese had approached the Russians and asked them to negotiate an end to the war.[69] The Russians didn't say anything about it, and we couldn't say anything about it because that would tell the Japanese we had broken their codes. However, the invasion was coming up near the end of the year. General Eaker was in the higher councils back in

---

[68] Less than a year after Germany's surrender in May 1945, Arnold was forced to retire due to heart trouble. In June 1946 he left Washington, D.C., and returned to his home in Sonoma, California, where he died on June 15, 1950. In 1949 Arnold was elevated to five-star rank as General of the Air Force by an act of Congress; he is the only Air Force or Army Air Forces air officer ever to achieve that rank.

[69] American cryptanalysts broke the Japanese codes, specifically the "Magic" diplomatic codes, before America's entry into World War II. For a history of how these codes were broken and then disseminated to American political and military leaders, see Ronald Lewin, *The American Magic: Codes, Ciphers, and The Defeat of Japan* (New York, 1982), 17–18, 60–69, 76–77, 280–291; Edwin T. Layton, *"And I Was There": Pearl Harbor and Midway—Breaking the Secrets* (New York, 1985). For the situation within the Japanese government on the decision to surrender, see Robert J. C. Butow, *Japan's Decision to Surrender* (Stanford, 1954), 142–210; Akira Iriye, *Power and Culture: The Japanese-American War 1941–1945* (Cambridge, Mass., 1981), 248–268; and Spector, *Eagle Against the Sun*, 545–550, 558–559.

Washington, and I have heard him many times say that President Truman made the decision to drop the bomb mainly on the estimates of the casualties we were going to get invading Japan.[70]

So we used the bombs. The war would have been over in time without dropping the atomic bombs, but every day it went on we were suffering casualties, the Japanese were suffering casualties, and the war bill was going up. As soon as we dropped the bombs, the Japanese switched to the Swiss, and about ten days later, we had a ceasefire. From that standpoint, I think use of the atomic bomb was a wise decision.[71]

Burchinal: From 8 August on there were 15 missions, and they ranged in size all the way up to as many as 1,000 planes, and we weren't taking any losses.

LeMay: I remember we had an Air Force Day. The Army had an Army Day, and the Navy had had a Navy Day for years—big celebrations—so we had an Air Force Day. I don't think I picked the day; somebody else picked it out. But on Air Force Day we celebrated: everybody goes today. We sent 850 airplanes up, I think with only about 20 aborts.[72]

---

[70] Gen. Ira C. Eaker (1896–1987), a native of Texas, was commissioned a second lieutenant in the U.S. Army Infantry in World War I. Quickly he decided to become a military pilot, achieving his wings in 1919. The 1920s were for Eaker a time of command, leading squadrons in the Philippines and New York; of study, (Columbia University for law); and of staff work, the Office of the Chief of the Air Service and the Assistant Secretary of War. In 1929, Eaker received a Distinguished Flying Cross for piloting the *Question Mark* on its famous 11,000-mile, 6-day flight that tested the feasibility of air refueling. In the 1930s he led air pursuit groups, attended senior military schools, and worked at Headquarters, Army Air Corps. By 1941, Eaker was one of a small cadre of air officers whom Arnold knew and trusted. In World War II, Eaker organized, trained, and led the Eighth Bomber Command before taking command of Eighth Air Force. From early 1942 to late 1943, General Eaker developed the forces, air tactics, targeting strategies, and coordinated plans for the American bomber offensive against Germany. In January 1944 Arnold assigned Eaker to be the Commander-in-Chief, Mediterranean Allied Air Forces. When the war ended Lt. Gen. Eaker became the Deputy Commander, Army Air Forces. He retired on August 31, 1947. Nearly thirty-eight years later, in 1985, Congress elevated Eaker to four-star rank in recognition of his contributions in winning World War II in Europe. James Parton, "*Air Force Spoken Here:" General Ira Eaker and the Command of the Air* (Bethesda, Md., 1986).

[71] The decision to drop the atomic bombs has been the subect of vigorous debate. For the history of decisionmaking within the United States government, see Louis Morton, "The Decision to Use the Atomic Bomb," in Kent Roberts Greenfield, ed. *Command Decisions* (Washington, 1960), 493–518; Martin J. Sherwin, *A World Destroyed: The Atomic Bomb and the Grand Alliance* (New York, 1975); Barton J. Bernstein, *Hiroshima and Nagasaki Reconsidered: The Atomic Bombings of Japan and the Origins of the Cold War* (Morristown, N.J., 1975); Carol S. Gruber, "Manhattan Project Maverick: The Case of Leo Szilard," *Prologue* 15 (Summer 1983): 73–87; Gar Alperovitz, *Atomic Diplomacy: Hiroshima and Potsdam* (New York, 1965).

[72] On August 1, 1945, Twentieth Air Force sent 836 B-29s over Japan. The largest element, 627 B-29s, bombed the Japanese cities of Hachioji, Toyama, Nagaoka, and Mito; the second element, 120 B-29s, struck the Kawasaki petroleum facilities; and the smallest element, 37

Kohn: All out of the Marianas?

LeMay: Out of the Marianas. Over 800 got to the target, and over 800 came home. We didn't lose an airplane even to accidents that day.

Catton: There were unique aspects to the campaign, General LeMay, that I think are worth remembering because I consider them historically important. First, there was the location of our bases, the Marianas. The combination of the B–29 airplane, and the location of the Mariana Islands, and the location of the enemy, were absolutely providential. The airplanes' range and payload were at a maximum flying from those islands. We were literally out of the reach of the enemy after the first few months, so we had a perfect setup, absolutely diametrically different from flying out of India into China, then out to the targets and then repeating the procedure to bring in our supplies. In the Marianas we had geography very much on our side. During the initial operations, with that long, 1,500-mile flight to the target and 1,500-mile flight back, we suffered mechanical problems because of the high altitudes at which we were flying and the loads that we were carrying. And enemy action hampered us. We lost airplanes. But once we captured Iwo Jima,[73] got "Mickey" Moore's fighters up there, and once we could take a full bomb load out of Tinian, Guam, and Saipan, we really had a tremendous setup to do the kind of things that bombers are able to do.[74]

B–29s, mined the Shimonoseki Straits and Nakaumi Lagoon. This combined strike was the largest single one-day bombing effort of the Pacific War. Carson and Mueller, *Combat Chronology 1941–1945*, 683.

[73] The battle for Iwo Jima, a small atoll lying midway between the Mariana Islands and Tokyo, began on February 19, 1945. It lasted for nearly 30 days and was one of the bloodiest amphibious landings and battles of the entire Pacific war. The U.S. Navy and Marines suffered 24,854 casualties—6,821 dead and 18,033 wounded. The Japanese defenders had proportionally even greater losses: of the estimated 23,000 Japanese soldiers and airmen defending Iwo Jima, only 213 were taken prisoner; the rest perished. Once taken by the Marines, the island became an air base for long-range fighters (P–51s) and an intermediate landing point for B–29s returning from bombing runs over Japan. From March to September 1945, more than 2,250 B–29s, carrying 24,761 airmen, made emergency landings on Iwo Jima. See George W. Garand and Truman Strobridge, *Western Pacific Operations* [History of the U.S. Marine Corps Operations in World War II] vol IV, (Washington, 1971) 443–738; Allan R. Millett, *Semper Fidelis: The History of the U.S. Marine Corps* (New York, 1980), 426–438; Richard F. Newcomb, *Iwo Jima* (New York, 1965).

[74] Maj. Gen. Ernest Moore (1907–), was a West Point graduate (1931) who led the Seventh Fighter Command onto Iwo Jima in March 1945. The Seventh had 222 P–51D long-range fighter escorts, 24 P–61D night fighters, and 111 P–47N day fighters. Moore had entered the Air Corps in 1932, specializing in pursuit. In the war he advanced within the Seventh Fighter Command from pilot to executive officer, assistant chief of staff for operations, operations officer, and commander. After the war, he served in the AAF's Continental Air Forces, at Headquarters USAF in Air Intelligence, and as the Commander of Thirteenth Air Force in the Philippines.

STRATEGIC AIR WARFARE

Burchinal: After the war, I went right from the Marianas to Japan and stayed for three or three and a half months with the strategic bombing survey. All the Japanese that we interviewed, including their top commanders, said that the war was over and would have ended prior to 1 November, the invasion date, without the atomic bomb. They said it was their realization that the military forces could no longer protect the Japanese people from destruction. One thing we haven't discussed is the aerial mining campaign that we ran out of the Marianas with the 313th Wing, which was one of the most successful that has ever been done anywhere.[75] In fact, we were starving Japan by late summer 1945, because all her ports were blocked with mines. They couldn't sweep them, they couldn't clear them, and it was a heck of a complementary effort as far as the forces were concerned.

Catton: Nothing moved through the Shimonoseki Straits, for example, for months before the end.[76]

Burchinal: Between the aerial mining and the bombing, we tore up the Japanese so much that they couldn't really move around. They were flat on their tail. They had had it, and they knew it. As Curt said, whom could they find to carry the message, and mediate?

Kohn: Apparently a major problem was whether the Japanese government could agree internally to seek peace, the politics inside the Japanese cabinet . . .

Burchinal: The A-bomb certainly gave them an excuse to come out of the closet, throw up their hands, and say . . .

Kohn: And go over the brink and go to the Emperor.

Burchinal: Yes.

LeMay: Let me relate an interesting sidelight on ending the war. When I

---

[75] The B–29 aerial mining campaign began in April 1945 and lasted until the Japanese surrender. The B–29s dropped some 12,000 mines on Japanese sea lanes, straits, and harbors. These mining operations, when combined with the impact of the Navy's submarines and aircraft, virtually paralyzed Japan's maritime traffic. See Craven and Cate, *AAF in WWII*, V, 662–674; Frederick M. Sallagar, "Lessons from an Aerial Mining Campaign," RAND Report R–1322 PR (Santa Monica, Calif., 1974).

[76] The Shimonoseki Straits separated the main Japanese islands of Honshū and Kyūshū. Because the straits were very narrow, at one point only one-fourth of a mile wide, Allied aerial mining, submarines, and naval shelling concentrated there, and forced Japanese commercial and military shipping to refrain from using the straits. In the first month of mining operations, more than fifteen Japanese ships using the straits were sunk or disabled. After March 27, 1945, no large Japanese warships attempted to pass through the Shimonoseki Straits. See Craven and Cate, *AAF in WWII*, V, 671–672.

72

arrived in India, I was under General Stilwell for administration and supplies, so I went to call on him.[77] He was not in his headquarters; he was out in the jungle someplace. I left a couple of cards, said hello to his chief of staff, and went back home. I didn't see Stilwell until he showed up in China one day when we were up there running a mission. He appeared right at the hot part. I said, "Come along with me until we get the mission off, and then we can sit down, and I can show you something." So he did. I spent perhaps six hours with him trying to explain what we were trying to do with bombers. Clearly I wasn't getting to first base; he just did not understand. He left and I never saw him again, except to wave when we boarded the *Missouri* for the surrender exercises. As soon as that was over, I got into the C-54 and returned to Iwo, looking at targets around in that area, and then went on back to Guam. A couple of days later, Stilwell, returning to the States through Guam, came over to see me. He said, "LeMay, I just wanted to stop and say hello and tell you that when I went through Yokohama to the surrender exercises, for the first time I realized what you were trying to tell me up in China. I was a language student as a second lieutenant in Yokohama, and I know what was there. When I saw what was left—then I understood."

The Late 1940s

Kohn: After the war, before General LeMay took over SAC, what was it like in the strategic business? What were the major problems in 1946 and 1947? General Johnson, you commanded SAC's Fifteenth Air Force. Was the problem not enough planes, too much demobilization?

Johnson: Of course, not enough planes and too much demobilization; yes.

---

[77] Gen. Joseph W. Stilwell (1883–1946) graduated from the U.S. Military Academy in 1904. Prior to World War II, he traveled and studied extensively in China, Japan, and the Far East. Early in the war, he was selected as commander of all U.S. Army forces in the China-Burma-India Theater and chief of staff to Gen. Chiang Kai-shek, leader of the Chinese Nationalist forces. When the Japanese defeated Chiang's Nationalist forces in 1942, Brig. Gen. Stilwell personally led the remnant army on a 140-mile forced march into the interior of China. In order to supply this Nationalist army, Stilwell asked the Army Air Forces to establish an airlift from India over the Himalayan Mountains to China. When General LeMay arrived in India in late August 1944 to command the XX Bomber Command, Stilwell had been promoted to four-star rank by President Roosevelt and was the Deputy Supreme Allied Commander of the China-Burma-India Theater under Adm. Lord Louis Mountbatten. See Charles F. Romanus and Riley Sunderland, *Stilwell's Mission to China*, Vol 1, in *U.S. Army in World War II: China-India-Burma Theater* (Washington, 1953); Tuchman, *Stilwell and the American Experience in China*, 256–349.

Demobilization was not a demobilization; it was a rout.[78] We just walked away and left everything. We started with nothing; I don't think we had a squadron left together in late 1945 or early 1946. We were starting to rebuild when I took over the Fifteenth, hoping to get more personnel and more crews and get the Air Force going again. We were expanding the force. George Kenney,[79] the SAC Commander, was actually not very active in running SAC. In my opinion he was busy on other things that were of interest to him, and he left most of his work to General McMullen, who was his chief of staff.[80] General McMullen had many ideas which I don't believe were really conducive to building an effective striking force. In his own mind it was what he wanted. He said, "I want to build a rounded officer. I am going to build officers for the future and not just troops right now to keep crews going." As

---

[78] On September 2, 1945, the day Japan surrendered, United States military forces consisted of 91 Army and 6 Marine divisions, 243 Army Air Forces groups, and 1,166 Navy combat ships. The United States had more than 12 million men and women in uniform. Less than two years later, on June 30, 1947, the Army, Army Air Forces, Navy, and Marines had fewer than 1.6 million people under arms. The Army Air Forces had decreased from a high point of 2,411,294 in 1943 to 303,614 in May 1947. Air combat strength had fallen precipitously from 243 groups in the war to 11 fully operational groups out of 63 authorized. Immediately after the war the pace of demobilization was so rapid that in one six-month period—September 1945 to February 1946—the Army Air Forces released 734,715 personnel. See Steven L. Rearden, *The Formative Years 1947–1950*, Vol 1, *The History of the Office of the Secretary of Defense*, I (Washington, 1984), 12; Herman S. Wolk, *Planning and Organizing the Postwar Air Force 1943–1947* (Washington, 1984), 117, 189, 213; and Craven and Cate, *AAF in WWII*, VII, 566–569.

[79] Gen. George C. Kenney (1889–1977) led the Strategic Air Command from March 1946 to October 1948 when he left to command Air University at Maxwell Air Force Base, Alabama. Kenney was a prominent American air leader who had commanded an aero squadron in World War I. He remained in the Air Service after the war, becoming an expert in aircraft technology and production. In World War II, Kenney won fame and four-star rank as Gen. Douglas MacArthur's air commander in the Southwest Pacific. In that role Kenney was a superb tactical air leader, an innovator, and an articulate spokesman for the role of air power in warfare. A prolific writer, General Kenney was the author of several books, including a reminiscence of his war experiences, *General Kenney Reports: A Personal History of the Pacific War* (New York, 1949; reprint, Washington, 1987).

[80] Lt. Gen. Clements McMullen (1892–1959) was both Chief of Staff and Deputy Commander of the Strategic Air Command from January 1947 to November 1948. A senior officer in the prewar Army Air Corps, McMullen was a rated pilot, an aeronautical engineer, and an expert in supply and maintenance. During World War II he was a general officer, serving in the United States and the Southwest Pacific. He commanded logistics, maintenance, and supply organizations and in 1944–45 worked directly for General Kenney as the Commander of the Far East Area Service Command. Following the war, Maj. Gen. McMullen was Chief of Staff for the Pacific Air Forces before moving to the Strategic Air Command. When Kenney became the SAC Commander in March 1946 he retained his former position as U.S. Military Air Advisor to the United Nations. He devoted most of his time and attention to the United Nations' position. Then in January 1947, Kenney named McMullen as his chief deputy, giving him wide latitude to run the command. McMullen reorganized SAC, changing its headquarters structure, personnel assignments, and training policies. For the situation within SAC in these years, see Harry R. Borowski, *A Hollow Threat: Strategic Air Power and Containment Before Korea* (Westport, Conn., 1982), 57–58.

Brig. Gen. Leon W. Johnson.
Courtesy Leon W. Johnson

the Fifteenth Air Force Commander, however, my job was to get the crews trained and create an effective combat force.

Burchinal: He had been on the logistics side of the house all his career up until then, hadn't he?

Johnson: I think he had, yes.

Burchinal: He commanded depots and that sort of business.

LeMay: One of the things General McMullen started was cross-training. Everybody had to be a pilot, a navigator, and a bombardier. As a matter of fact, he didn't have people trained in their primary specialty before he started cross-training them on something else.

Johnson: He made us cross-train before we were trained. I had been in personnel before I took the Fifteenth Air Force. I called in all the nonrated officers who were in the other services and who had been with us in the war. I tried to get them to come over to the Air Force. I promised them good careers. When I got to the Fifteenth Air Force, this program was working very well. I had a good engineering officer at Rapid City; I had good people generally. I received a call saying that we were only required to have twenty percent nonflying people in the Air Force; "You are over that, so get rid of these people." I rebutted it and rebutted it and also the cross-training policy

75

so much that when Roger Ramey, who commanded Eighth Air Force, came to see me at Colorado Springs, he said, "All you are doing is making Headquarters sore at you. Those people are not going to make any changes up there."[81] At SAC we couldn't do our mission very well. That was the thing, as I saw it anyway, and I think some of the others agreed.

Kohn: How did you understand your mission then, General Johnson? Did you look upon it as atomic warfare exclusively?

Johnson: I never gave a thought to it being atomic warfare only. I was just training the crews, getting them combat capable to do whatever they needed to do. I don't think we thought of ourselves as world destroyers or world savers or anything. We were given a job to do. I personally believe in disciplining units. I always believed that nondisciplined units were lousy; they never did a good job anywhere. I don't mean to emphasize strict discipline of the martinet type, but expecting people to do things they are supposed to do, when they are supposed to do them. That was all we were trying to do in the late 1940s: get the crews trained in their specialties, get the crews ready to be "marked," as Curt says, combat ready.

Catton: Let me give you a squadron commander's point of view. I was fortunate because I was in a high-priority outfit. We had the "SILVER PLATE" airplanes in the 43d Wing.[82] We underwent a very sharp reduction in manpower authorization in the fighting outfits, in the combat outfits. As a consequence, a crew member had to be ready to be another officer as well; that is what cross-training meant. But the problem was not only cross-training; there was a very substantial reduction in manpower levels that were

---

[81] Lt. Gen. Roger M. Ramey (1905–63) was a West Point graduate (1930) who served in the air force for 29 years. In the 1930s he was a pilot, operations officer, and commanding officer in pursuit units. He was in Hawaii on December 7, 1941, serving as commander of the 42d Bombardment Squadron at Hickam Field. Associated with the Pacific war from its inception, Ramey commanded bomb units from 1941–45. He commanded the 58th Bomb Wing (B–29s) in China and in the Marianas in 1944–45. He was one of General LeMay's wing commanders in the strategic air campaign against Japan. Immediately after the war, Brig. Gen. Ramey led the AAF Task Force that participated in the atomic bomb tests at Bikini Island in the Pacific. Firmly identified with strategic air warfare and the new atomic weapons, Ramey became a key figure in the new Strategic Air Command, serving as Commander, Eighth Air Force (1948–50). Subsequently, he served as Director of Operations, USAF, from 1950–54; Commander, Fifth Air Force, from 1954–56; and Deputy Commander-in-Chief, Continental Air Defense Command, from 1956–57.

[82] Catton, then a lieutenant colonel, was commanding the 65th Bomb Squadron (B–29s) in the 44th Bomb Group, 43d Bomb Wing at Davis-Monthan AFB, Arizona. SILVER PLATE was the code name for the B–29 bombers modified to carry twenty-kiloton atomic bombs of the type used at Hiroshima. By mid-1947, the Strategic Air Command had 160 B–29s on operational status, but only 27 were SILVER PLATE bombers.

Maj. Gen. Curtis E. LeMay.

available. General McMullen's theory was, "We can operate with smaller manpower authorizations and still get the job done. At the same time we will train officers for the future, to be versatile and able to do all kinds of things." It was destructive in terms of the flying proficiency of the organization.[83]

Johnson: He had one statement that is probably true. He said, "You can send 2,000 people out with no mission but to look after themselves, and they will be sending for aid before very long, and for more people."

Catton: That's right.

Kohn: General LeMay, did you talk to General Johnson on your way back from Europe in 1948 to take over SAC; did you stop in England and speak with General Johnson?

Johnson: No. I went to Wiesbaden to see General LeMay. I was working for

---

[83] At Headquarters, USAF, senior air leaders became so concerned about SAC's readiness that late in 1947 they asked Charles A. Lindbergh to examine the command's combat capability, especially that of the atomic units, and to suggest improvements. Lindbergh's report of September 1948 to General Hoyt Vandenberg, Chief of Staff, cited low standards of professionalism, personnel disruptions, and command training policies that "seriously interfered with training in the primary mission of the atomic squadrons." Within five weeks General Kenney had been reassigned and Lt. Gen. Curtis E. LeMay appointed as commander, effective October 19, 1948. Seven days later, Maj. Gen. McMullen departed, and Brig. Gen. Thomas S. Power became the new deputy commander. See Borowski, *Hollow Threat*, 53–71, 137–162.

him at that time. The Berlin Airlift was on when I was pulled out of the Fifteenth Air Force to go to England to set up a SAC bomber force there.[84]

I was actually in the CONUS in Spokane, Washington, when General LeMay was named SAC Commander. General Kenney met me there and said, "What are you doing here?" I said, "I am going to meet my master when he comes into my territory." Kenney didn't say anything. A few minutes later I was called to be in Washington, D.C. So I flew to Washington, then back to Colorado Springs, spent one night there, got set up in permanent change of stations, then flew all night to get up to Goose Bay, and then flew to Germany the next day to check in with Curt. He said, "What took you so long? I expected you on Wednesday." I had a permanent change of stations.

When I got home to Colorado Springs, I opened the door, and there was a shotgun standing by the door. I thought my wife had "gotten the word" ahead of me, but she had won it at bingo the night before, so it was all right.

LeMay: When I came back from Europe in 1948, I noticed the personnel situation that we have been discussing. When the war ended we were in the process of tearing the Air Force down. When we would disband an outfit, those that wanted out were sent to a processing station that got them out of the service. Those that wanted to stay in were usually ordered to a base somewhere close to their homes. It didn't make any difference whether the man was a fighter pilot or some other MOS [military occupation specialty]. The whole force was ill-manned. We didn't have the people we needed, and there were a lot of people we didn't need and couldn't use. The same was true of bases. Bombers were stationed at bases that had some other mission prior to the war, but if the base was to be kept, a bomber outfit was put there. Consequently, the warehouse would be full of supplies that pertained to something else, and not the supplies that bombers needed.

Then I took a look at the war plan; there was no war plan.

Kohn: Wasn't that one of the first questions that you asked General Catton on your first day as SAC Commander?

---

[84] Maj. Gen. Johnson went to England to command the Third Air Division in August 1948. General LeMay was then commanding U.S. Air Forces Europe, and the Berlin Airlift had been underway for eight weeks. The airlift began on June 26, 1948, in response to the Soviet Union's action which closed all road and rail traffic through the Soviet sector of Germany to the city of Berlin. On June 26 Gen. Lucius D. Clay, U.S. Military Governor, Germany, directed General LeMay to organize and conduct a limited airlift to resupply Berlin. That same day President Harry S Truman affirmed American support for Berlin and ordered the airlift accelerated to a full scale effort immediately. From that day until September 30, 1949, the Berlin Airlift brought 2,323,067 tons of food, fuel, and supplies to the beseiged city of 2,250,000. For the history of the crisis see Rearden, *Formative Years, 1947–1950*, 275–308; for a history of the airlift, see Tunner, *Over The Hump*, 152–224.

Catton: The first morning at Andrews Air Force Base, where SAC was headquartered, General LeMay said, "As the first order of business, I want to review the war plan."

Kohn: And there was no war plan?

LeMay: No. Then I asked about the status of training: "Let me see your bombing scores." "Oh," was the response, "we are bombing right on the button." They produced the bombing scores, and they were so good I didn't believe them. The same was true of the radar bombing scores. Then, looking a little further, I found out that SAC wasn't bombing from combat altitudes, but from 12,000 to 15,000 feet. I looked at the radar picture, and the planes weren't at altitude. There had been trouble with the radars working at altitude. Instead the crews bombed down where the radars would work. Instead of bombing a realistic target, they were bombing a reflector on a raft out in the ocean or in the bay down off Eglin Field. It was completely unrealistic.

It was perfectly apparent to me that while we didn't have very much capability, everybody thought they were doing fine. The first thing to do was convince them otherwise. So I ran a maximum effort mission against Dayton, Ohio—a realistic combat mission, at combat altitudes, for every airplane in SAC that we could get in the air. We had them all up, and not one airplane, not one crew, completed the mission as briefed: aborts all over the place, equipment that wouldn't work, the crews that didn't work, nothing worked. Afterward we got the commanders all together and laid it out: "Look at this."[85]

Catton: There were a lot of people in the command that weren't satisfied, General LeMay.

LeMay: I am sure there were, General Catton; however, the briefing I originally received indicated that everything was rosy.

---

[85] When this Dayton exercise began in mid-January 1949, every SAC flight crew received a prewar (1938) photograph of Dayton, which was indicative of the outdated air intelligence of cities in the Soviet Union. Then, every bomb group flew a mission against Dayton, simulating the bombing of industrial and urban targets from 30,000 feet. Bombardiers were directed to aim their radars on standard reflector targets. Bomb scores revealed that the simulated bombs fell in a range of 5,000 to 10,000 feet from the target, an unacceptable margin of error. LeMay later remarked, "You might call that just about one of the darkest nights in American aviation history." The significance of this failed exercise was that it revealed graphically the gap between SAC's training methods and the flying skills needed to carry out the mission of the nation's strategic air force. With only a limited number of long-range B–29 and B–36 aircraft and crews available, and the Berlin Crisis still unresolved, the poor performance by the SAC crew had far-reaching consequences. See Borowski, *Hollow Threat*, 167–168; Kantor and LeMay, *Mission With LeMay*, 433–34.

Johnson: We made that point. General LeMay asked, "What's wrong with SAC?" I replied, "I won't tell you. I have three young officers here with me who told you, and they mentioned cross-training." We were so busy fighting our headquarters and trying to get the training that we didn't have time to do anything else.

LeMay: That is another factor, a disease that headquarters is often liable to get: the belief that combat outfits are working for headquarters instead of headquarters working for the combat outfits. It takes a little doing once in a while to get that attitude changed, just in the matter of reports that come in. I had a system in SAC whereby about every three months we checked the reports that came in to see who read them and what they did with them if they were read. Often we would cut them out. The question was whether the staff was putting work on the combat outfits, or taking work away from the combat outfits so they could get ready to fight. With this as an illustration, the staffs would then get down to business.

We took the 509th Group, the original atomic outfit. I said: "Okay, we will start with that one." We cleaned out the supply warehouses and stocked the things that the unit needed. We equipped all the planes with the things they were supposed to have on them. Some of the airplanes didn't even have

Lt. Col. Jack J. Catton.
Courtesy Jack J. Catton

guns on them; since it was peacetime, they supposedly didn't need them, and didn't have them. We put all the things on the airplanes they were supposed to have, and then started cleaning out the people that didn't belong there, and getting people in who did.

Kohn: Was that a bloody process? Do you all remember that?

Johnson: Oh, boy! I remember it vividly.

Catton: There is a point that needs to be made. During this period of time, when General LeMay came back from the airlift and just before General Johnson went over to Europe, we had a very minimal atomic delivery capability—very few airplanes, less than a hundred. The Fifteenth Air Force had none, for example. The Eighth Air Force had the 509th, the 43d, and the 7th, and those were the only atomic-capable outfits. Those outfits were given attention different than the rest; they had their weaponeers trained, and they had their bomb commanders trained. What we didn't have was brought out when General LeMay took charge. That is, we did not have a war plan for the use of those forces. All of us in the outfits at the operating level were just assuming: "Yes, at the higher levels things are well planned, and we just have to be well trained to execute." I learned that was not the case. The day that

Col. David A. Burchinal.

was bloody was the first day or two that General LeMay was there. You correct me, sir, where I go astray, but I have got to say that you were so disappointed and frustrated with what you found in the Strategic Air Command when you came back to command it, that it got right bloody. General LeMay assembled the staff and advised who was going to stay and who was going to go. He restaffed himself right then. So it was bloody, but it was necessary and appropriate, and we really got a head of steam going.

LeMay: I even found group commanders who were not checked off on their airplanes.

Johnson: I want to go back to an important point. When we demobilized the Air Force, I was in personnel and we were making plans for an orderly demobilization. I remember being over at the railroad station trying to figure out how many troops could be carried by the railways from San Francisco to various parts of the country as the men came home from the Pacific. General Muir Fairchild was sitting there. "What if the people demand to get out," he asked? We said, "Well, gee, the plan won't work." The men did demand to get out immediately, and I let them out. All of this helps explain the condition of the Air Force at the time. Another example: the records of my wartime group were left on the floor up at Rapid City, South Dakota. Some of them were gathered up and sent to the Pentagon when I was there; but in general there was no one left even to keep the records of the units from World War II. We started from nothing, from nothing, to rebuild the Air Force. I think this helps explain this lack of readiness all the way through.

Kohn: How did you conceive of warfare in that period before the Korean War? When General LeMay took over SAC and found no war plan, you must have begun to think through war plans and discuss the subject with the Joint Chiefs. General Burchinal, you were down at Air University then. Was that being discussed?

Burchinal: No. We were reviewing history at that point. We weren't looking ahead; we were looking back and seeing what happened, and teaching from what happened—the basic lessons, that sort of thing. I don't think we fully realized what nuclear supremacy meant that early. It was probably well into the 1950s before the full dawning of what supremacy in the nuclear field really meant to us and how much of a ticket we could write based on that supremacy. We came to realize we had supremacy—after General LeMay came in and made SAC a fighting force again.

Johnson: I think we realized what supremacy was, but no one wanted to use it or even think about using it. Orvil Anderson gave a lecture, if you will remember, a talk at Air University about going after the Russians, and he was retired in about three days by President Truman.[86]

Burchinal: Very fast. We knew we had supremacy, and we knew what we could do with it, but no one wanted to start another war. We had just finished one. We saw nothing bothering us right at that time worth the cost. Curt certainly went to work and made a very effective, efficient force very quickly when he got back.

Catton: Maybe this will put it a little bit into perspective, and you will all remember this. Once General LeMay got back (we are always pointing at this man, but that is natural), we went to work. We not only started developing a war plan for the use of the forces that we had, but we developed a programming plan—the first time I learned about programming—how we were going to build the force.

What was our concept of warfare? A good question. Remember, General LeMay, the Pegasus exercise down at Montgomery? Remember J. B. Montgomery and the briefing in which we showed the Air Force how we could use our forces, how we could stage through, pick up bombs at the general AEC storage sites, then fly to our prestrike staging bases, and finally to the targets that we would hit?[87] We convinced everybody that we knew how to do it and that, in fact, we could do it. It was at that time, vivid in my memory, that we achieved recognition on the part of the Air Force of the primacy of strategic nuclear warfare. That was the first hurdle that had to be overcome. Do you remember that?

---

[86] Following the invasion of South Korea by North Korea in June 1950, Maj. Gen. Orvil A. Anderson, Commandant of Air War College, gave a series of lectures, briefings, and press interviews describing how he believed the United States should use its strategic air forces to launch a preventive strike on the Soviet Union. These remarks, along with similar ones by Secretary of the Navy Francis P. Matthews, alarmed President Truman and his advisors who were then in the midst of defining, conducting, and limiting America's participation in the Korean War. When Truman addressed the nation on radio on September 1, 1950, he declared explicitly that the United States "did not believe in aggressive or preventive war." The next day, Gen. Hoyt S. Vandenberg, Chief of Staff, USAF, relieved General Anderson of his position and declared that the Air Force's primary mission was "prevention of war." Shortly thereafter, General Anderson retired. *New York Times*, September 2, 1950, pp 1,4,8.

[87] As a result of the disastrous Dayton exercise, General LeMay asked General Montgomery, SAC's Director of Operations, to develop detailed operational war plans that would assign specific targets to each SAC bomb crew and aircraft. That war plan, SAC Emergency War Plan 1–49, became the basis for all SAC training, force structure, and to a degree, future force requirements. The "Pegasus" briefing by General Montgomery was at the Air War College in 1949. This briefing was one of many that SAC leaders gave in the late 1940s and early 1950s in their attempt to explain how they intended to wage strategic air warfare. See Borowski, *Hollow Threat*, 167–168, 170–185; David Alan Rosenberg, "American Atomic Strategy and the Hydrogen Bomb," *Journal of American History* 66 (1979): 62–87.

Johnson: I remember that, but I disagree to this extent. I think all of us understood the mission, that SAC certainly had priority over everything in all of our minds. I had served enough places and positions in those years to see that. SAC had the mission, really, to deter. We didn't want war; we wanted to deter war, and the atomic force was going to deter the war.

LeMay: Let me tell you what I was trying to do. I remembered the horrible experience that we all had during the war, of going to war with nothing, with no training and having to start from scratch. With the atomic weapon, we could not afford this kind of unpreparedness again. My goal was to build a force that was so professional, so strong, so powerful that we would not have to fight. In other words, we had to build this deterrent force. And it had to be good. So I got guys who knew something about doing this, and we got busy and did it.

Kohn: Was there a sense in 1948 and 1949, when you first took over, that war was imminent? What with the Berlin Crisis, the Czechoslovakian coup, the deterioriating situation in China. . . .[88]

LeMay: No. There may have been that sense back here in Washington, but to my mind there was only a possibility of war. I was sitting at Wiesbaden as USAFE Commander in 1948, an hour-and-a-half drive from the Russian border, and not a single doughfoot between me and the border. I remembered a couple of guys called Kimmel and Short—at Pearl Harbor.[89] So I got busy

---

[88] From 1947 through 1949 a rapid series of international crises worsened the relationship between the Soviet Union and Western nations. In 1947 Communist guerrillas in Greece and Turkey were challenging existing national governments in civil wars. Poland and Hungary had fallen firmly under Soviet influence. In China, Communist armies led by Mao Zedong were challenging the Nationalist government. In 1948 the government of Czechoslovakia was taken over by Communists who quickly adopted a Soviet-style constitution. North Korea closed its borders to United Nations observers and established firm economic and diplomatic ties with the Soviet Union. Then in June 1948, the Soviets closed all surface travel to Berlin and the Western nations responded with the Berlin Airlift. While the Berlin Crisis lasted well into 1949, several of the other crises reached their conclusions: in China the Red armies defeated the Nationalists and seized power; in Greece the government defeated the Communist guerrillas. During 1949 the United States government learned that the Soviet Union had detonated an atomic device. These post-World War II events and the comcomitant political, economic, and military policies of the Soviet Union and the Western democratic states created what is known today as the Cold War. For a review of the issues on the origins of the Cold War, see John Lewis Gaddis, "The Emerging Post-Revisionist Synthesis on the Origins of the Cold War," and the responses, in *Diplomatic History* 7 (1983): 171–204. A recent bibliographical listing of the major literature is Ralph B. Levering, *The Cold War*, 1945–1987, 2d ed., (Arlington Heights, Ill., 1988), 199–212.

[89] Adm. Husband E. Kimmel (1882–1968) and Lt. Gen. Walter C. Short (1880–1949) were the Navy and Army commanders at Pearl Harbor on December 7, 1941, the day of the Japanese surprise attack. Both were relieved of duty, recalled to Washington, and suffered through eight separate presidential, congressional, and military investigations. The first, authorized by

and did what I could. I established my own private NATO, operating with airfields stocked back behind the Rhine, and things of that sort. But I really didn't believe we would have a war.

As a matter of fact, General Trudeau, who commanded the constabulary, and I concocted a plan where he would run a small military force up the autobahn and open Berlin by force.[90] I would have a communications van, and when he started up, I would have the B–29s based in England in the air over Germany with the fighters that I had also moved up closer. If General Trudeau made the decision that he was at war, instead of just pushing through token resistance, then I would let the air force go and hit the Russian airfields. The Russians were all lined wingtip to wingtip on their airfields. We presented this plan to General Clay, the High Commissioner for Germany, and he sent it to Washington, but the answer was "No."[91] Well, Monday morning quarterbacking indicated later that had we done that, the fracas would have ended right there. There would have been no opposition. Everybody agrees to that now, I think, but we didn't do it, and we fell back on the airlift.

When we started the airlift I only had one squadron of DC–3s over there. We needed more and more, and I added all the administrative airplanes. Finally it dawned on me what we were trying to do, so I had a talk with Clay and said, "Look, if you really want to do this job, I have got to have some help. Let's get some MATS people and the four-engine airplanes over here and really get going on it." We did, and we opened up some more airfields and really got going on the problem.

Johnson: I told my staff over in England that if they ever jammed that homer

---

President Roosevelt and headed by Supreme Court Justice Owen J. Roberts, declared in January 1942 that Kimmel and Short displayed "bad judgment" and "dereliction of duty" in not defending Pearl Harbor against Japanese attack. Both men retired from the service. See Gordon Prang, *At Dawn We Slept: The Untold Story of Pearl Harbor* (New York, 1981); Martin M. Melosi, *The Shadow of Pearl Harbor: Political Controversy over the Surprise Attack, 1941–1946* (College Station, Tex., 1977); Roberta Wohlsetter, *Pearl Harbor: Warning and Decision* (Stanford, 1962).

[90] Lt. Gen. Arthur G. Trudeau (1902–) was a West Point graduate who entered the Infantry. In World War II he led Army combat units in North Africa, Northern Europe, and the Pacific. In 1948 General Trudeau was commanding the U.S. Army's First Constabulary Brigade in Berlin.

[91] Gen. Lucius D. Clay (1897–1978), was the Military Governor of the American zone of occupied Germany from 1946 to 1949. As the senior military official in Germany at the time of the Berlin Crisis, Clay worked directly with the Joint Chiefs of Staff, the Secretaries of Defense and State, and the President. He also met with his counterpart from the Soviet Union, Marshal Vasiliy D. Sokolovsky. Upon his retirement in 1950, General Clay wrote his memoirs, *Decision in Germany* (Garden City, N.Y., 1950). For a history of the political-diplomatic context of the Berlin Crisis see Rearden, *Formative Years, 1947–1950*, 272–308.

85

in Berlin, the Russians were serious. The Russians weren't serious as long as they left that homer there.

Kohn: What was the homer?

Johnson: The beacon that planes homed in on to land at Berlin.

Kohn: The beacon at the airfield?

Johnson: Yes, right near it.

LeMay: We established a procedure going in to Berlin. Everybody went in on instruments regardless of the weather; even if there was not a cloud in the sky, they still used that same procedure. Everybody went in just exactly alike, using the homer. We had a GCA [ground controlled approach] there, too, I guess, at the time.

Johnson: Yes, sir. The whole point is the Russians knew how to jam. They jammed anything they wanted to jam, but they didn't dare move that far. I knew they weren't serious unless and until they jammed that beacon.

Korean War

Kohn: Did the Korean War have an impact on SAC? Perhaps we did not really mount a strategic campaign in Korea in the same manner we waged strategic warfare in World War II. You controlled all the strategic airplanes, General LeMay, at that time.

LeMay: Not when they left and went to Korea.[92]

---

[92] Nine days into the Korean War, Gen. Hoyt Vandenberg, Chief of Staff, USAF, directed the movement of two medium bomb groups (22d and 92d) from the United States to Japan. Vandenberg thought that these two SAC B–29 units would be effective in Korea in flying air interdiction missions against the enemy's long supply lines, which stretched the length of the peninsula into South Korea. Simultaneously, General Vandenberg directed Lt. Gen. George E. Stratemeyer, Commander of the Far East Air Forces, to organize and establish a Far East Air Forces Bomber Command (Provisional). To that command he assigned the two SAC B–29 units, plus the 19th Bomb Group (B–29s), already in the Pacific Theater. To command, General Vandenberg selected Maj. Gen. Emmett "Rosie" O'Donnell, Jr., then a SAC numbered air force commander. In late 1950 the 22d and 92d Bomb Groups returned to the United States. Two other SAC bomb groups, the 98th and 307th, which had gone to Korea in August, remained with the Far East Air Forces Bomber Command. Throughout the war, SAC B–29 aircraft and crews were rotated to the theater and assigned to the Far East Bomber Command. See Robert F. Futrell, *The United States Air Force in Korea, 1950–1953* (New York, 1961; rev. ed., Washington, 1983), 46, 71.

Catton: There was one B–29 outfit on Okinawa, the 19th, that belonged to the Far East Air Forces. It did not belong to General LeMay. He owned the rest until the war started.

LeMay: When we got orders to send them over there, we picked the low-priority outfits, the lowest ones on the totem pole.

Kohn: Why did you choose the low-priority units?

LeMay: Because I did not want to destroy the capability that we had built up for a strategic war if we had to go to war. We sent the outfits that were not fully manned and not combat ready for the overall strategic war plan.

Catton: All the wings that he sent over there were not nuclear-capable.

Kohn: Did you believe our bombing campaign against North Korea was strategic air war as you knew it?

LeMay: No, we never did hit a strategic target.

Catton: It was interdiction.

Kohn: It was interdiction with strategic bombers?

Catton: Absolutely. The strategic targets—the resources—were located north of the Yalu, yet we were not permitted to go north of the Yalu.[93] General LeMay kept very close contact with those three units—the 98th, the 92d, and the 22d. He kept very close tabs on those outfits; they did the jobs they were asked to do extremely well. He also sent Rosie O'Donnell to be the FEAF Bomber Command Commander. So, while General LeMay did not relinquish possession of those outfits, they were under the operational control of the theater commander. Right?

LeMay: Right.

Kohn: No lessons to be learned from the strategic standpoint, then?

---

[93] The Yalu River forms the border between North Korea and the Chinese province of Manchuria. When the war began, the Truman administration did not allow American and Allied aircraft to fly north of the Yalu River in order to avoid provoking China. The fear was that China, if attacked, would enter the war allied with North Korea. After the Chinese intervention in November 1950, the Truman administration maintained its policy restrictions on air forces flying north of the Yalu River in order to limit the war to the Korean peninsula. See Harry S Truman, *Memoirs: Years of Trial and Hope* (New York, 1956), 374–389, 394, 433; Robert J. Donovan, *Tumultuous Years: The Presidency of Harry S Truman 1949–1953* (New York, 1982), 299–300, 307–310, 342; Rosemary Foot, *The Wrong War: American Foreign Policy and the Dimensions of the Korean Conflict, 1950–1953* (Ithaca, N.Y., 1983), 88–130.

STRATEGIC AIR WARFARE

LeMay: How not to use the strategic air weapon.

Kohn: Could you expand on that a little bit, General LeMay?

LeMay: Right at the start of the war, unofficially I slipped a message in "under the carpet" in the Pentagon that we ought to turn SAC loose with incendiaries on some North Korean towns. The answer came back, under the carpet again, that there would be too many civilian casualties; we couldn't do anything like that. So we went over there and fought the war and eventually burned down every town in North Korea anyway, some way or another, and some in South Korea, too. We even burned down Pusan—an accident, but we burned it down anyway. The Marines started a battle down there with no enemy in sight. Over a period of three years or so, we killed off—what— twenty percent of the population of Korea as direct casualties of war, or from starvation and exposure?[94] Over a period of three years, this seemed to be acceptable to everybody, but to kill a few people at the start right away, no, we can't seem to stomach that.

Burchinal: I think there was one thing learned: that SAC could deploy fast, that forces could be brought from the United States if there were bases prepared for them. Bombers could be brought to bear very rapidly. I believe that led to bases in North Africa, bases in England, and the rotation concept. SAC could deploy very rapidly.[95]

---

[94] The Korean War lasted 3 years and 1 month. South Korea had a population of 20,189,000 in 1950; it suffered approximately 3 million civilian and 225,000 military casualties. North Korea had 9,600,000 people in 1950; it had approximately 1,300,000 civilian and military casualties. R. Ernest Dupuy and Trevor N. Depuy, *The Encyclopedia of Military History* (New York, 1986), 1251; Tai Sung An, *North Korea: A Political Handbook* (Wilmington, Del., 1983), 33.

[95] In these years, 1950–60, American military strategy was rooted in a national policy of containing Communism and a military policy of deterrence and retaliation against aggression. As articulated in a series of war plans developed in the late 1940s, SAC's strategic bombers and support forces would be based in the United States but flown to staging bases in Great Britain, Iceland, Newfoundland, Alaska, Guam and other places in preparation for operations against targets in Eastern Europe, the Soviet Union, and China. Shortly after their creation, these war plans were refined; the changes stipulated prepositioning a certain portion of SAC's bombers, tankers, supplies, and people overseas at the staging bases on temporary duty. There they trained, stood combat alerts, and were ready to strike quickly when ordered. By 1957 SAC had 30 bases overseas, located in the United Kingdom, Spain, Morocco, Greenland, Newfoundland, Labrador, Puerto Rico, and Guam. In 1956 a review of this prepositioning policy by RAND demonstrated that the Soviet Union had the capability of launching crippling air and missile strikes against SAC's overseas staging bases. According to this analysis, SAC's forces overseas were extremely vulnerable to attack. Partly for this reason, and because of two other factors— reductions in Air Force budgets and the operational feasiblity of using all-jet air-to-air refueling of the bomber forces—the practice of temporarily basing large numbers of strategic forces abroad was reconsidered and in the early 1960s substantially curtailed. In subsequent years, all SAC nuclear forces returned to the United States. See John L. Gaddis, *Strategies of Containment* (New York, 1982), 89–127; Bruce L.R. Smith, *The RAND Corporation* (Cambridge, Mass., 1966), 195–240.

B–29 Superfortresses drop bombs over a target area during the Korean War.

LeMay: We had to deploy in order to fight with the airplanes we had in those days. So we developed a plan for it and the equipment for it and practiced it. For instance, we had what we called "flyaway kits" that contained essential spare parts. We kept them up-to-date because as the airplanes aged, the parts in the flyaway kit changed a little bit. Different parts would be needed, different quantities of parts, but we were up-to-date so if we had to go, you just slammed the lids, and went. The boxes were all marked; some went on the bomber, others went with the first transports that came in to move the ground echelon over. Practicing that, we could deploy an outfit very rapidly. As a matter of fact, I deployed an outfit once so quickly that the crews and the people in the air echelon didn't even go home to pack a bag. Later on we ironed it out so we could plan our deployments and tell our people, "You are going over on a deployment on such-and-such a date. You are going to come back on such-and-such a date, and you can take some leave along in this period and have some time with your family." It took a little doing because the Air Staff was shuffling people without any regard to personal comfort or practicality.

Catton: Even in the early days, we had the capability in our higher priority outfits to operate nearly autonomously, given an airfield, out of our flyaway kits. We were quite highly mobile and mobility-trained. We exercised that capability frequently.

SAC in the 1950s and Early 1960s

Kohn: In the 1950s, as SAC was building up, how did you determine your force requirements: your targeting, and the structure of your force? Were you building up with as much as you could get, to create the strongest possible deterrent? Did SAC discuss force structure with the Air Staff . . .

LeMay: I don't think we thought too much about the structure of the force. It was pretty well set in concrete—what the force was going to look like and what each individual group looked like. We had a training plan that was rigidly followed. We had a war plan of how we were going to fight the war.

Kohn: Was the plan your own, or did it come from Washington?

LeMay: It was ours. There wasn't anything that came out of Washington. As a matter of fact, I don't think we got anything out of Washington other than maybe a little guidance on targets that should be hit. We did the plan right up till the time I left in 1957.[96]

Catton: The center of gravity for planning the use of the SAC force was at SAC—no place else. It developed that way because the expertise was there, and that was pretty well recognized in Washington, both by the Air Staff and JCS. Don't let the lessons learned in World War II go unremembered; the reason we were as successful as General LeMay made us, certainly in the Pacific, was because we were a specified command and the responsibility for achieving the objectives of that command lay with the commander in chief of that specified command. The first specified command was Twentieth Air Force:[97] we learned that lesson very, very well. Korea was an anolmaly.

---

[96] For a perspective on American nuclear strategy, war plans, and their formulation in the late 1940s and 1950s see Lawrence Freedman, "The First Two Generations of Nuclear Strategists," and David MacIssac, "Voices From the Central Blue: The Airpower Theorists," in Peter Paret, ed., *Makers of Modern Strategy: From Machiavelli to the Nuclear Age* (Princeton, 1986), 624–647, 735–778; Gaddis, *Strategies of Containment*, 3–126; Borowski, *Hollow Threat*, 163–185; David Allen Rosenberg, "American Atomic Strategy and the Hydrogen Bomb Decision," *Journal of American History* 66 (1979): 6287; Rosenberg, " 'A Smoking Radiating Ruin at the End of Two Hours': Documents on the American Plans for Nuclear War with the Soviet Union, 1954–1955," *International Security* 6 (1981–82): 3–38; Melvyn P. Leffler, "The American Conception of National Security and the Beginnings of the Cold War, 1945–1948," *American Historical Review* 89 (1984): 346–381.

[97] The term "specified" command is a post-World War II term. In that war, American forces deployed overseas came under the command of a theater or area commander. In early 1944, however, Army Air Forces leaders argued successfully that the B–29 strategic forces being developed for the Pacific Theater should be controlled not by the theater commander, but by the Joint Chiefs of Staff. Their reason was to insure unity of command over all strategic bombing

Should we not say something about the nuclear capability we had available within a very few hours to the Far East commander?

LeMay: Yes, go ahead.

Catton: We never used strategic concepts in Korea. However, available to General MacArthur and later General Ridgeway, was the atomic capability of a unit of the 43d Wing which we put on the island of Guam, at Andersen Field.[98] Those were B–50As, atomic capable.[99]

General LeMay provided through Gen. Thomas S. Power, originally the SAC X-ray commander in Tokyo, the wherewithal to provide MacArthur with atomic weapons if the President decided to use them.[100] We could have atomic weapons very reliably and very accurately delivered within a period of

---

forces in order to carry out the strategic bombing campaign against Japan, and to avoid diversion of the bombers to support ground and naval operations. Their logic was accepted, and the JCS authorized establishment of the Twentieth Air Force. This precedent became important in the postwar years. In December 1946 President Truman approved a JCS "unified" command plan which set up eight commands: seven overseas theater commands (Far East Command, Pacific Command, Alaska Command, Northeast Command, Atlantic Fleet, Caribbean Command, and European Command) and one specified command, the Strategic Air Command. Under this structure, the commanders of each of these regional or functional grouping of forces reported to the Joint Chiefs of Staff. At first, the term "specified" was not well defined and it was not until 1951, in the midst of the Korean War, that the JCS clarified the term to mean a JCS command with the same operational and command arrangements as a unified command but which consisted essentially of forces from only one military service. See Rearden, *Formative Years*, 135–136.

[98] Both Gen. Douglas A. MacArthur and Gen. Matthew B. Ridgeway served as Commander-in-Chief, United Nations Command, during the Korean War. General MacArthur led UN forces from June 1950 to April 1951, while General Ridgeway commanded the same forces from April 1951 to May 1952.

[99] B–50A bombers entered SAC's inventory in February 1948. These B–50As were a derivative of the B–29 bombers used so extensively in World War II. The newer bombers had more powerful engines, redesigned nacelles, and a new, stronger and lighter wing structure. Between 1948 and 1955, there were as many as 260 B–50s and RB–50s (reconnaissance) in SAC's operational forces. Because the B–50s could fly long distances (up to 4,900 miles, unrefueled) at high altitudes (up to 36,000 feet) and were capable of carrying a large bomb load (up to 10,000 pounds), they were part of the United States' first line of strategic bombers in the late 1940s and early 1950s. See Swanborough and Bowers, *United States Military Aircraft Since 1909*, 91–95, 101–112.

[100] Maj. Gen. Thomas S. Power was SAC's Vice Commander (1948–54) and at this time the general officer in charge of the command's atomic forces in the Far East. In the midst of the Korean War, General LeMay set up a system of commands, each named for a letter in the alphabet spelled out phonetically, to control SAC's forces and weapons deployed overseas. The first two commands, X-ray and Zebra, were located in Japan and Great Britain respectively. In 1952 the phonetic command system was expanded to control all SAC nuclear forces allocated to support the unified theater commanders. By 1954 SAC had five phonetic commands: X-ray (Far East), Victor (Alaska), Yoke (French Morocco), Zebra (United Kingdom), and Oboe (Northeast Atlantic, Newfoundland, and Greenland). See Futrell, *Ideas, Concepts, and Doctrine*, 217; Rosenberg, " 'A Smoking Radiating Ruin,' " *International Security* 19.

about sixteen hours. We exercised that capability constantly throughout the war, of course on a simulated (but very realistic) basis, using iron bombs and so on. In those cases we depended not only on radar but also on a very fine SHORAN [short-range navigation] capability that we immediately put into that outfit's B–50s. That capability was there to be used and would be highly effective if our national command authority chose to do so.

LeMay: I might add something about the atomic bombs at this time: the military services didn't own a single one. These bombs were too horrible and too dangerous to entrust to the military. They were under lock and key of the Atomic Energy Commission. I didn't have them, and that worried me a little bit to start with. So I finally sent somebody to see the guy who had the key. We were guarding them. Our troops guarded them, but we didn't own them.

Catton: They didn't trust us.

LeMay: Civilian-controlled completely.[101] I remember sending somebody out—I don't know whether it was Monty[102] or somebody else—to have a talk with this guy with the key. I felt that under certain conditions—say we woke up some morning and there wasn't any Washington or something—I was going to take the bombs. I got no static from this man. I never had to do it or anything, but we had an understanding.

Kohn: Do you remember at all who the man was or when this occurred?

LeMay: I don't remember.

Catton: I don't, either. There was a very complicated transfer procedure from the Atomic Energy Commission to SAC.

Kohn: Do you remember when this was, General Catton?

LeMay: It was pretty early in the game.

Kohn: 1948–49?

---

[101] In 1946, the President proposed and Congress authorized the establishment of a civilian-controlled Atomic Energy Commission. The law explicitly transferred the Manhattan Project's property, personnel, and records to the new commission. The legislative intent at the time was to insure civilian control over nuclear weapons policy, research and development, production, and storage. See Richard G. Hewlett and Oscar E. Anderson, Jr., *The New World, 1939–1946,* [*A History of the United States Atomic Energy Commission*, vol I] (University Park, Pa., 1962–1969), 620–680; David Allan Rosenberg, "U.S. Nuclear Stockpile, 1945 to 1950," *The Bulletin of Atomic Scientists* 38 (1982): 25–29.

[102] Maj. Gen. John B. Montgomery was Director of Operations at Headquarters SAC from 1949 to 1951.

Catton: Yes. We did not have custody of the weapons until 1950 or 1951. There were so many hurdles to negotiate before you could get to a target that it was ridiculous, and the weapons transfer—you had to go where the weapon was, pick it up . . .[103]

LeMay: And take it to the combat zone. We had to set up the transports to do that.

Johnson: Curt, I don't think you are saying that you could have started the war?

LeMay: No, absolutely not. If we got into a position where the President was out of action or something else turned up, I was going to at least get the bombs and get them to my outfits and get them loaded and ready to go—at least do that much.

Johnson: You couldn't release them, however.

LeMay: I would have, under certain circumstances, yes.

Johnson: You mean after we had already been attacked?

LeMay: If I were on my own and half the country was destroyed and I could get no orders and so forth, I wasn't going to sit there fat, dumb, and happy and do nothing.

Johnson: I wanted the country half-destroyed before you would contemplate this.

LeMay: I may not have waited until half the country was destroyed, but I felt I had to do something in case no one else was capable of doing anything.

Johnson: If we were under attack—that sort of thing.

LeMay: Yes, if we were under attack, and I hadn't received orders for some reason, or any other information.

---

[103] General Montgomery, SAC Director of Operations, stated in an oral history interview that in 1948–49, if the President had issued an order to launch an attack, SAC's small, atomic-capable bomb group based at Roswell Field, New Mexico, (509th Composite, B–29s) would need five or six days to depart the base, fly to an Atomic Energy Commission storage site, load the bombs, and fly to a forward base before launching air strikes against the enemy. See Borowski, *Hollow Threat*, 103–104, 110. Gordon Dean, Chairman of the Atomic Energy Commission, stated that during the Korean War, on April 6, 1951, President Truman authorized the transfer of nine nuclear weapons to the Air Force. This transfer was the first time the military had direct control of nuclear weapons since World War II. See Roger M. Anders, ed. *Forging the Atomic Shield: Excerpts from the Diary of Gordon E. Dean* (Chapel Hill, 1987), 137–144.

Johnson: In response to their attack?

LeMay: I was going to take some action at least to get ready to do something. Lacking orders and lacking the assumption that I was going to get some in the near future, I would take some action on my own.

Catton: This business, of course, as you can understand, had progressed from nearly no capability to deliver atomic weapons to the absolute necessity of being able to launch within very brief periods of time, within the warning time available. Eventually, of course, we got to where we are today, and we have been there for quite a while. SAC finally got custody of the weapons. We were finally authorized to load them on ground alert. We were finally authorized to take them into the air, for example, on airborne alert. We made tremendous progress, of course, because the real facts of life demanded that the responsibility be delegated to SAC. However, to return to General Johnson's nervousness, the launch and execution procedures of the strategic forces are absolutely inviolable. You just cannot attack with atomic weapons without the proper kind of authority. This is very carefully safeguarded through all the procedures that were developed.[104]

Kohn: Was General LeMay talking about an earlier time, when those processes were being developed and there was great uncertainty?

LeMay: Oh, absolutely.

Johnson: I just don't want anything said here to indicate to some casual reader that General LeMay could start a nuclear war, or anybody else could, by himself. Once I asked an Italian colonel down on a Jupiter missile in Italy if he would be able to fire that missile even if he was deranged (I was checking for General Norstad).[105] The colonel lit into me, saying that his family went back to 1200 AD and there had never been anyone deranged in all those years. I did not know whether Curt has that long a family history—or if I do, either!

---

[104] In the mid-1950s, SAC installed explicit "positive control" procedures throughout the command, along with new communications technologies linking the President to CINCSAC and to the operational forces. These procedures were further enhanced by the addition in the 1960s of electronic locking devices called "permissive action links," which prohibited the accidental or unauthorized arming of nuclear weapons. These procedural and technological developments are discussed in Paul Bracken, *The Command and Control of Nuclear Forces* (New Haven, Conn., 1983), 179–237; Bruce G. Blair, *Strategic Command and Control* (Washington, 1985), 68–69, 283, 286, 249–257; Richard H. Kohn and Joseph P. Harahan, eds. "U.S. Strategic Air Power, 1948–1962: Excerpts from an Interview with Generals Curtis E. LeMay, Leon W. Johnson, David A. Burchinal, and Jack J. Catton," *International Security* 12 (1988): 78–95.

[105] Gen. Lauris Norstad was the Supreme Allied Commander, Europe and Commander-in-Chief, U.S. European Command from 1956 to 1963.

LeMay: I haven't been interested enough to trace my family back that far either. What I am trying to say is that SAC was the only force we had that could react quickly to a nuclear attack. It did not make much sense to me to be in a position of not being able to act because I had no weapons. We had no idea of what confusion might exist, or who the president might be, or where, if a bomb hit Washington. I see nothing to be gained by discussing under what conditions I would have taken action in case of the destruction of Washington and loss of contact with the government. I doubt if I would have retaliated if Washington were the only target hit. But I certainly would not have waited until half the country were destroyed. The main thing is that by making agreements to get the weapons we had some options rather than having none at all.

Kohn: During the 1950s did you feel that you had adequate information to wage a campaign against the Soviet Union, if it came to that? Historians are interested in how we viewed the target structure, what we knew of Russian warmaking capability, and the deployment and disposition of their military forces. When some people talk about the era of massive retaliation, they assume that all SAC was going to do was wipe out every Russian city and the Russian population, rather than attack Russian military forces.

LeMay: Let me talk about that a little bit. To start with, when I first came back from Germany, there wasn't any doubt in my mind that if we had to go to a full-scale war we would use nuclear weapons. That was the capability we worked on, to go to nuclear weapons. We didn't consider any unit really combat ready unless it had a nuclear capability. Of course, we didn't have very many bombs at the beginning. The stockpile was rapidly growing of course, but we had a small number to start with.[106]

There was a time in the 1950s when we could have won a war against Russia. It would have cost us essentially the accident rate of the flying time, because their defenses were pretty weak. One time in the 1950s we flew all of the reconnaissance aircraft that SAC possessed over Vladivostok at high

---

[106] The number of American atomic weapons and SAC bombers for the years 1946–50 were as follows:

Year	Weapons	Nuclear Modified Aircraft
1946	9	23 (December)
1947	13	23 (January)
1948	50	58 (December)
1949	unknown	225 (December)

Source: Rearden, *The Formative Years*, 439; Rosenberg, "U.S. Nuclear Stockpile, 1945–1950," *Bulletin Atomic Scientists*, 25–30.

noon. Two reconnaissance airplanes saw MiGs, but there were no interceptions made. It was well planned too—crisscrossing paths of all the reconnaissance airplanes. Each target was hit by at least two, and usually three, reconnaissance airplanes to make sure we got pictures of it. We practically mapped the place up there with no resistance at all. We could have launched bombing attacks, planned and executed just as well, at that time. So I don't think I am exaggerating when I say we could have delivered the stockpile had we wanted to do it, with practically no losses. Of course, that has changed now, but that was the condition that existed in the 1950s.

Catton: I don't think we ever had any great concern about being able to execute the mission from the standpoint of enemy action throughout the 1950s. We were quite confident that we could do that. Our problems were more operational, rather than the threat of being shot down by flak or fighters.

LeMay: We were planning on a nuclear war. Then as time went on—the Korean experience for instance—it began to dawn on us that we might get some restrictions on the use of atomic weapons.

Kohn: We have been talking almost exclusively about planning and flying operations. What was it like to be a wing commander in SAC in the 1950s?

Catton: Very exciting.

Johnson: It was first-rate.

Burchinal: The best job around.

Catton: A SAC wing commander—and there is a bias showing here—I think was the most sought after position in the Air Force. Do you agree, David?

Burchinal: Yes. Even when I first got back to SAC, my first job was with the 40th, the last B–29 outfit in SAC.[107] We were down low on the seniority totem pole; as soon as I would get a crew trained, they would pull it and assign it to one of the higher priority outfits. I was a replacement training center! The last B–29 went into storage out of the 40th!

Catton: Salina, Kansas?

Burchinal: Yes.

---

[107] From 1953 to 1954 General Burchinal, then a colonel, commanded the 40th Bomb Wing, a B–29 unit stationed at Smoky Hill AFB, Kansas.

Kohn: But it was an exciting time.

Johnson: It was.

Burchinal: Even operating as a sort of replacement center was good.

Kohn: You had good people, a strong sense of cohesion, tremendous élan?[108]

Catton: We gained great satisfaction from knowing we had an absolutely vital mission, that we were well led, and that the country was completely dependent on our succeeding in our mission. That feeling permeated down to the wing commander and throughout the crew force. Just as in World War II, as General Johnson has mentioned, the outfit looked to the commander for leadership. They got it, or he didn't stay very long.

Burchinal: You had a sense of purpose—that was the whole thing.

Kohn: Was it difficult because it was peacetime, or was there no sense of peacetime in SAC . . .

LeMay: It was wartime.

Catton: Training in SAC was harder than war. It might have been a relief to go to war.

Burchinal: To go from the 40th over to the 43d was a real switch for me, from the lowest to one of the highest priority outfits in SAC.[109] We were involved in deployment, because we were on our ninety-day TDYs over to North Africa and England at the time. You are right, it was war. It was a twenty-four-hour, seven-day-a-week job, and you didn't look upon it as anything else.

Kohn: Was General LeMay a presence in the whole command?

Burchinal: You better believe it

Kohn: Would you expand on that?

Burchinal: Say the name again. . . . I can always remember—at least it was attributed to General LeMay—that he once said, when somebody got fired,

---

[108] Within the Air Force, SAC was considered to be an elite command. It had a certain spirit, which was depicted, along with the pressures of working under constant nuclear alerts, in three contemporary Hollywood films: *Strategic Air Command* (1955), *Bombers B–52* (1957), and *A Gathering of Eagles* (1963).

[109] The 43d Bomb Wing (B–47s) was based at Davis-Monthan AFB, Arizona.

"I can't afford to differentiate between the incompetent and the unfortunate."

Catton: He was somewhat "less than tolerant" for failure to perform.

LeMay: We checked all of these things, all the time. We had a team go out. They would take off from Offutt, clear for one base but land at another, and hand the commander a letter: "Execute your war plan."

Burchinal: Then we got into "No-notice." In other words, you would go into a period where orders might come to your wing without warning. All of a sudden, the word would come through; you went to the airplane, and you took off—twelve airplanes out of the wing. You flew a profile of your combat mission. You would do a radar-bombing attack, perhaps from Tucson, on a target in France. Then you would land in England, and you would come on back. You might do this a couple of times. You never did pack a bag for that; you had the bag packed, stored down in operations.

Johnson: I want to inject something here—I think I mentioned it casually before—Curt earned all his commands. He progressed by good work from the bottom up. I don't think he knew as many people as some of the rest of us

Brig. Gen. O. Ohman, Commander, 36th Air Division, congratulates Col. David Burchinal, Commander, 43d Bomb Wing, immediately after Burchinal landed the 1st B–47 assigned to the 43d Wing, while Mrs. Burchinal and daughter Wendy look on.

Brig. Gen. Catton stands before a B–52 at Homestead Air Force Base, Florida, on occasion of his flying his 10,000th hour. Courtesy Jack J. Catton

knew, perhaps not as many, but every job he held he performed so well that everyone enjoyed working for him.

Burchinal: He wrote the book as he went along.

Johnson: I don't want to praise him because he might get big-headed.

LeMay: I picked people out that could do the job, and the person knew the job he had to do. Then I got out of his way and let him do it. He either did it, or he didn't. If he did it, fine; if he didn't, I got somebody else.

Catton: From the early 1950s the wing commander was required personally to brief the numbered air force commander every time the wing received a change to the war order. Wing commanders personally would brief their numbered air force commander on his war plan. The wing commander knew that war plan. He knew his targets. He knew every detail about the war plan because he personally had to brief his boss, and of course, the numbered air force would brief the commander. So we were involved.

Burchinal: You lived with your crews and the war plan all the time. You were always being briefed by your crews on their particular target.

Catton: They briefed you, the wing commander, and then you briefed the numbered air force commander.

LeMay: Along that line, during the war, it was standard thinking in the combat units that the next higher echelon of command didn't know what the hell they were doing. In many cases they had a point. In our war plan in SAC, I would bring somebody in from the unit who participated in the war plan so that a wing knew that somebody from its outfit had participated in the war plan. Thus people in the wings had more confidence in the plan, that it was the best plan that we possibly could devise with what we had at the time.

Kohn: What was your reaction to the intercontinental missiles?[110] You all had grown up in the Air Force flying airplanes. You viewed yourselves as pilots. But here people were developing these ground machines. Was there opposition in the Air Force to missiles? Did you personally feel any?

Catton: I think there was apprehension more than opposition. We were not sure whether missiles were going to replace airplanes, or supplement them. More than opposition, I think we wanted to be shown the reliability and the performance capability of the new weapon. Having said that, SAC indeed pushed hard for ICBMs, as well as for IRBMs.[111] Wasn't that your experience?

Johnson: I believe so. Personally I was so delighted when I saw the *Time* cover years ago with 25 missiles on it that I said, "Gee, it won't be long before we can all quit worrying and go out and play golf." However, we really knew

---

[110] In the 1950s and 1960s the Air Force, Army, and Navy developed eight ballistic missiles: Jupiter, Thor, Atlas, Titan I and II, Minuteman I and II, and Polaris. Of these, the Air Force deployed operational units of Thors (1958), Atlases (1959), Titan Is (1962), Jupiters (1961), Titan IIs (1962), Minuteman Is (1962), and Minuteman IIs (1965). The Strategic Air Command had operational responsibility for almost all of these new units. See J. C. Hopkins, "The Development of the Strategic Air Command, 1946–1981," (Office of the Historian, Headquarters, SAC, 1986), 77–135.

[111] In the early 1950s the Air Force, Army, and Navy were developing ballistic missiles. Terminology identifying these missiles centered on range; ICBMs were intercontinental ballistic missiles with ranges in excess of 5,000 miles. The IRBMs were intermediate-range ballistic missiles with a range of approximately 1,500 miles. The Air Force, because of its strategic mission, was assigned development of ICBMs. The Army and Navy had joint responsibility for development of IRBMs until 1956, when Secretary of Defense Charles E. Wilson directed in a policy memorandum that the Air Force would research, develop, deploy, and operate all land-based ICBMs and IRBMs. The Army was restricted to deploying and operating ballistic missiles to a range of 200 miles, while the Navy was assigned development and deployment of all ship-based IRBMs. See Loyd S. Swenson, Jr., James M. Grimwood, and Charles C. Alexander, *This New Ocean: A History of Project Mercury* (Washington, 1966), 23–25; Edmund Beard, *Developing the ICBM, A Study in Bureaucratic Politics* (New York, 1976), 196–197.

better. As the old wrestling coach used to say, "There ain't no hold that can't be broke."

LeMay: I never quite felt that way. I was glad to get missiles. As a matter of fact, some of those things were started back when I was in charge of R&D on the Air Staff. But look at it from the crews' standpoint: they had practiced, practiced, and practiced. We had dropped atomic bombs; we knew what we could do with them. We have never as yet fired a missile with an atomic warhead on it. I think the Navy did one once, but that's all. We have never fired a missile with an atomic warhead on it. In other words we have never gone through the whole cycle. So there is always some question: will they work? We have done everything humanly possible to ensure that they will, and they probably will, but we have never done it. Here again, in the back of one's mind, is that first outfit going into combat the first time and screwing up the mission. We practiced in SAC. We ran our war plan time and time again. The crews spent hours and hours and made hundreds of bomb runs on

Composition of 42d Bomb Wing, January 1956, representative of a typical SAC Bomb Wing in the 1950s:		
Unit	Officers	Enlisted
Hq 42d Bomb Wing (B–47s)	53	133
69th Bomb Squadron	97	202
70th Bomb Squadron	95	207
75th Bomb Squadron	99	194
42d Field Maintenance Sqdn	8	539
42d Periodic Maintenance Sqdn	5	166
42d Armament & Electronics Maintenance Sqdn	9	379
42d Air Refueling Squadron	103	207
42d Tactical Hospital	28	117
4034th USAF Hospital	18	13
Hq 42d Air Base Group	59	299
42d Operations Squadron	8	175
42d Supply Squadron	14	305
42d Motor Vehicle Sqdn	5	188
42d Air Police Sqdn	5	308
42d Food Service Sqdn	2	280
42d Installation Sqdn	7	241
524th Air Force Band	0	16
	615	3,969

Source: Strategic Air Command, History of 42d Heavy Bomb Wing, January 1, 1956-January 31, 1956.

their target in the trainer. So we had confidence, but we didn't have quite that same confidence in the missiles. Because having them added to our deterrence capability, we wanted them, we took them, and we used them. There wasn't any opposition from any place on it. To this day I think everybody has one reservation: we have never shot a missile under war conditions.

Kohn: Did you have trouble integrating them into the force? Were there specific problems that you remember?

Burchinal: The early Thors and Jupiters[112] were, of course, integrated with the overseas forces, the forces that were on TDY. As I recall we covered all their targets with manned airplanes initially; Thors and Jupiters, I think, were all backed up with manned airplanes.

Johnson: Yes.

Burchinal: One never counted on them as an independent strike force sufficiently reliable in themselves.

LeMay: The accuracy of the first missiles was nothing to jump up and down about, either.

Catton: Think about this for a moment. I remember when General LeMay pulled me into the headquarters the second time to do requirements, and I got my first briefing on something called Atlas.[113] Christ, I had come from the 43d Wing, and we were still working real, real hard to bring our celestial navigation CEP down, so that we would be sure of a good radar fix, and hit

---

[112] The Thor was developed in the mid-1950s as an intermediate range ballistic missile. Thor missiles could project a nuclear warhead approximately 1,900 miles. Between 1959 and 1965, the British Royal Air Force had three squadrons of the American-developed Thor missiles. Each RAF squadron had 20 missiles. The Jupiter was another American-developed intermediate range ballistic missile which was deployed in Europe, in single squadrons in Italy and Turkey. Beginning in 1961, the U.S. Air Force jointly operated these thirty-missile squadrons with the air forces of the host nations. The Jupiters were liquid-fueled missiles with a range of approximately 1,900 miles. By the end of 1963, both the Thors and Jupiters had been withdrawn from Europe.

[113] The Atlas was a liquid-fueled, intercontinental ballistic missile with a range of approximately 5,000 miles. It was a large missile, 75 feet high and 10 feet in diameter, and was armed with a single warhead. Developed by a special USAF management team led by Maj. Gen. Bernard A. Schriever, the Atlas had the highest priority of any weapon developed and fielded during the Eisenhower administration. Begun in January 1955, the Atlas was rushed from research and development to operational status in three years and three months. The Strategic Air Command activated its first Atlas missile wing at Francis E. Warren AFB, Wyoming, in 1958. From that time forward the number of Atlas ICBMs increased steadily, until December 1962 when there were 142 in SAC's missile force. For a few years, these Atlas missiles were the bulwark of the nation's ICBM deterrent force. Then in the 1960s, SAC's missile force gained the more advanced Minuteman and Titan II missiles. By June 1965 all of the Atlases had been removed from the active force.

Launch of an Atlas ICBM from Vandenberg Air Force Base, California.

the target—all that good stuff.[114] These idiots pulled me down into the basement there and started explaining to me that we were going to shoot this rocket, that was going to go 5,000 miles and it was going to be within—what the hell did we have then—I guess about a mile of the target.

LeMay: About a mile or two miles.

Catton: About a mile circular error. There you are, shooting a rocket like a cannon, and it is going to go 5,000 miles and be within a *mile* of the aiming point. That was just hard for me to comprehend. That makes you apprehensive. Then there was General LeMay's point about being tested fully, and being *sure* you know what you are doing. I don't know how the ICBM could have gotten more momentum behind it than was given by SAC.

---

[114] CEP is an acronym for "circular error probable." It is a term to describe accuracy: one-half of all shells, bombs, or missile warheads will fall within a specified radius of a circle centered on the target. Thus, a one-mile CEP would mean that one-half of all the weapons aimed at a specific target or point would fall within one mile of that target.

Kohn: How about air refueling? Were there any problems there?

Catton: The first real capability was with the B–50s. Remember, when "Jim" Gallagher made the around-the-world trip, those tankers were KB–29s equipped with hoses.[115] I was General LeMay's requirements guy, and I was supposed to be half-smart. He called me in one day. He called me Catton (he called me that for about seven or eight years). "Catton," he said, "what do you think about air refueling as a capability we could put into the force?" I, in my brilliance and foresight, said, "General LeMay, I think refueling is a unique capability that we should perfect so we can use it in very specialized circumstances. We never should plan on broad use of it throughout the force." That's how I got to be a general!

Burchinal: What did he respond?

LeMay: I kind of agreed with him at the time.

Catton: Thank you, General LeMay.

LeMay: At that time we had those hoses trailing out of the tankers.

B–50 being refueled by a KB–29 tanker.

---

[115] On March 2, 1949, Capt. James C. Gallagher and his 14-man crew flew a B–50A, dubbed the "Lucky Lady II," on the first nonstop, round-the-world flight. The flight lasted 94 hours and 1 minute and covered 23,452 miles. The B–50 was refueled in the air 4 times by KB–29 tankers, which were specially modified B–29 aircraft. In contrast, less than a year earlier, 2 SAC B–29s, the "Lucky Lady" and "Gas Gobbler," flew around the globe in 15 days, stopping enroute 8 times. Hopkins, "Development of the Strategic Air Command, 1946-1981," 14–18.

Burchinal: I remember that hose—the English probe and drogue.[116]

LeMay: The bomber came up behind the tanker with a grappling hook and flew across the hose hoping the hook would snag the hose; then you pulled it in and got it hooked up and transferred your fuel. Mark Bradley decided he could do better than that, and he came with the boom.[117]

A B–29 tanker-aircraft (above) is refueling at high speed a B–50 Superfortress medium bomber through the flying boom.

---

[116] At this time there were three basic inflight refueling techniques, each involving a tanker aircraft flying ahead and above the receiving aircraft. The earliest method, developed by Alan Cobham of Great Britain, had the crew of the tanker aircraft shoot a hose from a harpoon-like device across the wing of the trailing aircraft. Once the hose was caught on a hook, it was reeled in and attached to an interior fuel tank. The second method, called the probe and drogue system, had the tanker trail out a hose with a cone-shaped receptacle called a drogue. The receiver aircraft, equipped with a nozzle-shaped probe, flew it into the drogue and the fuel flowed into the receiving aircraft's interior fuel tanks. This method was used in the Korean War to refuel F–84 jet fighters. The third method, the flying boom, was devised by Brig. Gen. Clarence S. Irvine (SAC), Brig. Gen. Mark E. Bradley (Air Material Command), and Cliff Leisy (The Boeing Company). It differed by having the fuel transferred from the tanker by means of a long telescoping pipe—a boom—which was guided into a receptacle on the receiver aircraft by a specially trained boom operator. In the 1960s the flying boom refueling method became standard throughout the Air Force.

[117] Gen. Mark E. Bradley (1907–) was a graduate of West Point (1930) who entered the Artillery Branch, but switched to the Air Corps, learning to fly at Brooks and Kelly Fields, Texas. A fighter pilot, Bradley became in 1937 a test pilot at Wright Field, Ohio. Before World War II he was the P–47 project officer, shepherding the aircraft through testing and development into production. For much of the war Bradley remained at Wright Field as Chief of the Fighter Branch and Flight Test Section. In 1945 he went to the Pacific theater, serving as Chief of Staff, Fifth Air Force. An experienced aeronautical engineer, Bradley returned to Wright Field after the war and worked on refueling technologies for extending the range of bombers and fighters. Successful, he moved into senior leadership positions at Headquarters USAF in the 1950s and subsequently, in 1962, became the Commander of the Air Force Logistics Command. He retired in 1965.

Then, when we got the B–47, an airplane which would not reach the number one target even from advanced bases, we had to have refueling.[118] Fortunately, there was some redundancy built into the thing, and we got the range increased and started getting more out of the engines that we had. We were planning on about sixty hours on the engines when we bought them, and we bought a whole flock of engines for the B–47s that we never used because in later versions we increased the engine usage tremendously.

Catton: They never wore out.

LeMay: Needing tankers for the B–47s gave us the impetus to spend the money for a tanker force. Then Boeing, of course, with some advanced thinking on their own, produced the KC–135 [119]—the commercial 707—as a

B–47, SAC's first all-jet bomber.

---

[118] The B–47 was the Air Force's first all-jet bomber. Built by Boeing, the first flight of the XB–47 was in December 1947, and the first production model, the B–47A, arrived at SAC in October 1951. The range of the jet bomber was 4,000 miles. Boeing built 2,041 B–47s for the Air Force and they were used in a variety of missions: medium-range bombing, photo-reconnaissance, weather, and finally as target drones. In the early 1960s, the B–47s were phased out of operation, with the last bomber leaving SAC in 1966. See Marcelle S. Knaack, *Post-World War II Bombers, 1945–1973* (Washington, 1988).

[119] The KC–135 derived from developmental work done by Boeing on the famous commercial jet airliner, the 707. Produced for the Air Force by Boeing, the KC–135 was the Air Force's first all-jet tanker aircraft. Its first test flight was on August 31, 1956, and less than a year later it became operational in SAC (June 28, 1957). Capable of offloading 120,000 pounds of fuel, the KC–135 had a range, depending upon the fuel load, in excess of 3,000 miles. Boeing built several variations of this aircraft for the Air Force's specialized missions: electronic reconnaissance, airborne command and control, electronic warfare, and military airlift. In all, the Air Force acquired 820 KC–135s and 45 C–135s. In 1981 SAC began a lengthy program to modernize the KC–135 fleet, equipping approximately one-half of the tankers with new engines and other modifications which are planned to extend the life of each aircraft by an estimated 27,000 flying hours (and the usage of the fleet to the year 2020). See Peter Bowers, *Boeing Aircraft Since 1916* (New York, 1968), 348–376; Kenneth Munson and Gordon Swanborough, *Boeing* (New York, 1971) 112–115; John W. R. Taylor, ed., *Jane's All the World's Aircraft, 1985–1986* (London, 1986), 365–366.

KC–135 tanker.

tanker. Of course, it made a good transport, too, but they did it on their own, and we immediately bought that airplane with the boom. The boom produced a different ballgame altogether.

Catton: We had the KC–97s with the boom first, and that was great, but to get a jet airplane to refuel a jet bomber force was *really* "arriving."[120]

LeMay: The KC–97 wouldn't fly fast enough to keep the B–47 from stalling when it had a full load of fuel. So in order to fuel, you had to dive the KC–97 to get up enough speed so that the bomber could get full and not stall off the boom.

Catton: Even before that, you had to make the rendezvous. The KC–97s were operating at about 12,000 to 14,000 feet, and the B–47s up at 33,000 to 37,000 feet. The rendezvous was quite a trick, because you had to make a very precise descent to come out behind your tanker, go up to observation position, and grab—but we did it. We really did well.

Burchinal: You didn't waste any time once you got down to low altitude because you were burning fuel so fast.

Catton: Yes. The KC–135 was a tremendous step forward because we were at jet altitudes and at jet speeds. The B–52 behind the KC–97 was a real lousy

---

[120] The KC–97 tanker was the military counterpart of the famous Boeing Stratocruiser airliner of the early 1950s. Like the commercial airliner, the KC–97 (tanker) and the C–97 (cargo) flew transoceanic and transcontinental distances (4,300-mile range). These aircraft entered the Air Force in July 1950, principally as refueling tankers for SAC's bombers and escort fighters. In all, the Air Force acquired 592 KC–97 tankers. Bowers, *Boeing Aircraft Since 1916*, 305–313.

arrangement.[121] The B–52 was a harder airplane to handle and much heavier. It was a bad match. But refueling really made SAC, because with the B–47s we would have had to do an awful lot of forward staging to get to any targets at all. The B–36 was the only airplane in the interim that had the necessary range.[122]

Kohn: Let me go back to strategic policy for a moment. Did the "Massive Retaliation" policy of the 1950s mean that we planned only to fight a general nuclear war?

LeMay: There are as many answers to that question as there are people around, I guess. But I think too many people thought of massive retaliation as automatically pushing all buttons, shooting all guns, that sort of thing in response to virtually anything the Russians did. Nobody that I knew in the military ever thought of it that way. Massive retaliation I think was a word coined by either newspapermen or some public affairs guy someplace in the military. The idea was to have overwhelming strength so that nobody would dare attack us—at least that was my idea of it, and what I attempted to accomplish out at SAC—that we would have such strength that we would never have to do any fighting.

Catton: I sure agree with the boss. Massive retaliation was a phrase that did not describe what we intended to do at all. The important thing, of course, was always to be able to prevail at the highest level of intensity, so that any kind of an escalation would be to the disadvantage of the enemy.

Certainly as the Air Force and the country were building SAC's capability, we intended to be able to operate across a much larger portion of the warfare spectrum. Now I am just talking SAC, but from the Air Force

---

[121] B–52s began service with the Air Force in June 1955. They were all-jet, heavy bombers capable of carrying 28,250 pounds of bombs over an unrefueled range of 6,000 miles. Carrying a crew of six, the B–52 went through eight major design models before the Air Force purchased in 1962 the last of the 722 strategic bombers. Still in operational service in SAC in the late 1980s, the B–52 holds the distinction of remaining operational longer than any other bomber in Air Force history. See Knaack, *Post-World War II Bombers*; Bowers, *Boeing Aircraft Since 1916*, 337–347; Jeff Ethell and Joe Christy, *B–52 Stratofortress* (New York, 1981).

[122] The B–36 was a product of the Army Air Forces' long-range planning just prior to World War II. The requirements stipulated that the B–36 would be a strategic bomber capable of flying transoceanic distances. Prior to and during World War II, the B–36's development was preceded by the B–17, B–24, and B–29 bombers; consequently, it did not go into production until 1947. Between 1947 and 1959 the Air Force acquired 382 B–36 bombers; all were assigned to the Strategic Air Command. Despite the fact that no B–36 ever flew in combat, the bomber's range of 7,500 miles and its payload of 72,000 pounds, made it a crucial part of the nation's deterrent forces in the early 1950s. The B–36 was one of the largest aircraft ever built, with a wing span of 230 feet, a length of 162 feet, and 10 engines. Andrew W. Waters, *All the U.S. Air Force Airplanes, 1907–1983* (New York, 1983), 104–105.

point of view, we certainly intended to be capable across the entire spectrum. The degree of capability to fight at different parts or portions of the spectrum is what really matters.

Burchinal: Of course, we didn't have that much capability in other parts of the Air Force in the early to mid-1950s. We had it mostly in SAC.

Catton: "Massive" referred to what we could do proportionately to what the Russians could do to us. We had nuclear supremacy over the Soviets—such substantial nuclear superiority that it was massive in relation to what they could bring to bear on us. I surely agree with General LeMay, that it was not just pushing all the buttons in sight. There was a very clear targeting philosophy and a very professional war plan for SAC to go to war. In those early days in the 1950s, SAC was about the only war force we possessed.

Kohn: Was your war plan—and here I only want to speak in general terms, of course—always for a substantial strategic campaign in the World War II sense?

LeMay: No. We had a total war plan, and that was virtually the only thing that was planned. However, it was so segmented that you had a lot of choices over what could be done—something less than that if that was the choice you wanted to make. The main thing was that this force was not built simply for retaliation: That is, "If you don't behave, we are going to hit you with all this." It was built for people to see, and looking at it, nobody would want to tackle it. That was our main objective—what we hoped would happen, and what did happen.

Johnson: I have recently heard this referred to as that "immoral" policy of massive destruction. My goodness, it was not immoral! No one ever expected it to have to be used. That was its whole purpose. As Air Deputy of Europe in the late 1950s, people asked me how many airplanes the Russians had in Berlin. I replied, "I don't know, and I don't care because they are not going to move because we have superiority." Personally I never expected, and it was the farthest thing from my mind, that we would ever have an attack on the United States as long as we had that strength.

Burchinal: There were some similarities to World War II, in that we were not trying to hold cities hostage by means of a terror threat, or anything like that. We were targeting, if push came to shove, what was important militarily and what was important economically to him in supporting his military. So there was that carry-over from the strategic concepts of World War II.

Kohn: When the Kennedy administration took office, was there much of a change in the nature of our forces, our strategy, our planning, our capabilities, our targeting? They enunciated a very different policy—flexible response—but it doesn't sound like it changed our forces.[123]

Burchinal: Let's look at it this way: (Robert) McNamara was not fond of the Strategic Air Command or its capabilities.[124] As a matter of fact, he didn't approve any substantial improvements or new weapons for SAC in his budgets, except for the SR-71 for reconnaissance.[125] He was the one who sold out the British strategic air forces when he denied them the Skybolt missile, because he wanted to have Britain and France actually stand down their nuclear forces so there would be a bipolar nuclear world.[126] He thought that would be much simpler to manage.

---

[123] "Flexible response" was the name the Kennedy administration adopted for its military policy. As articulated by Secretary of Defense Robert S. McNamara and Gen. Maxwell D. Taylor, who was both the Military Representative to the President (1961–62) and Chairman of the Joint Chiefs of Staff (1962–64), this policy called for the expansion of U.S. ground, naval, and air forces so that they would be capable of fighting wars of various kinds, conventional and nuclear, at different levels of conflict, from low-intensity guerilla wars all the way to general nuclear war. See William W. Kaufman, *The McNamara Strategy* (New York, 1964), 51–55; Maxwell D. Taylor, *The Uncertain Trumpet* (New York, 1961), 130–164; Lawrence Freedman, *The Evolution of Nuclear Strategy* (London, 1981), 228–244.

[124] Robert S. McNamara (1916–), the Secretary of Defense in the Kennedy and Johnson administrations, was strongly identified with three issues: exerting civilian managerial control over the separate military services; implementing the new military policy of "flexible response" and the force structure required to carry it out; and, shaping the United States' military policy in the Vietnam War. During McNamara's tenure from 1961 to 1968 he restructured the nation's nuclear forces by revising nuclear strategy, adding more submarine ballistic missiles and intercontinental ballistic missiles, reducing reliance on strategic bomber forces, and initiating programs to modernize the command and control networks linking the President to the strategic deterrent forces. See Henry L. Trewhitt, *McNamara* (New York, 1971); Kaufman, *McNamara Strategy*; and James M. Roherty, *Decisions of Robert S. McNamara: A Study of the Role of the Secretary of Defense* (Miami, 1970).

[125] The SR-71 "Blackbird" was a supersonic reconnaissance aircraft designed and produced by Lockheed in the early 1960s. Capable of flying over 2,000 miles per hour at altitudes as high as 85,000 feet, the SR-71 has become one of the United States' principal manned reconnaissance platforms. See Jay Miller, *Lockheed SR-71* (Arlington, Tex., 1985); Richard P. Hallion, *Test Pilots: The Frontiersmen of Flight* (New York, 1981), 240–244.

[126] The Skybolt missile was an air-to-ground nuclear missile with a range of approximately 800 miles. Originally developed by the Air Force in the mid-1950s, the Skybolt was supported strongly by the British who wanted it for the RAF Vulcan bombers. Because of the Vulcan's slow speed and large radar signature, it could not penetrate Soviet air defenses; but with the Skybolt it would be capable of striking at Soviet targets from standoff distances. In 1962, Secretary McNamara cancelled the Skybolt program, citing escalating costs and the technological success of another missile, the Minuteman. Shocked, the British made the Skybolt cancellation one of their discussion points at the December 1962 Bermuda Conference, attended by Prime Minister Harold M. Macmillan and President John F. Kennedy. There, McNamara stated the American position forcefully, and President Kennedy reaffirmed the cancellation decision. In the later 1960s the British government turned away from bombers and began acquiring submarines equipped with ballistic missiles. See Trewhitt, *McNamara*, 172–178; Kaufman, *McNamara Strategy*, 124–125, 219–227; Richard E. Neustadt, *Alliance Politics* (New York, 1970), 30–55.

Johnson: I know that when I briefed him in Paris—the last thing I did on active duty over there—about the Europeans coming in with their conventional forces, McNamara said he wanted the British to put in more. I said, "We have been trying to get them to put in more, and they won't do it. And I can understand why, personally." He said, "Well, make them." That was his concept: we would make these people do these things. Well, they haven't put them in yet as far as I know.

Catton: You know, Dick, I think it might be helpful to look at these policies from a different point of view: massive retaliation and SAC seem to be synonymous in some people's minds (wrongly, but it is the case); flexible response seems to imply the rest of the military in a conventional, down-to-guerrilla-warfare sense. I think we ought to remember that we had a Department of Defense—I should say the military services, one of which was the Air Force. SAC was *the* major war-fighting capability of the Air Force

President John F. Kennedy and Air Force Chief of Staff Gen. Curtis E. LeMay at a firepower demonstration at Eglin Air Force Base, Florida, May 1962.

and of all the services for quite awhile, because the capability was there. The potential was there, and the capability was developed by virtue of the emplacement of resources. When flexible response became the Kennedy administration policy, what we are really saying is that instead of adding resources to Strategic Air Command, we put resources elsewhere, across the spectrum of war-fighting capability, in tactical forces. It is important that we consider this from an Air Force point of view, not just SAC.

LeMay: To go back to your question, "Was there any drastic change when the Kennedy administration came in?" The administration spouted new phrases and things of that sort, but as far as the Air Force was concerned, we had no radical change in thinking at all. We were all on the same track. However, the Kennedy administration thought that being as strong as we were was provocative to the Russians and likely to start a war. We in the Air Force, and I personally, believed the exact opposite. While we had all this superiority, we invaded no one; we didn't launch any conquest for loot or territory. We just sat there with the strength. As a matter of fact, we lost because we didn't threaten to use it when it might have brought advantages to the country.

Catton: I think we all know, and it might be redundant, but it ought to be said: When you talk about massive retaliation, you are talking, as General LeMay expresses it, about "real strength." The concept of strength was absolutely proved, and dramatically, during the Cuban Missile Crisis, when we had absolute superiority.[127] Khrushchev was looking down the largest

---

[127] The Cuban Missile Crisis began in mid-October 1962 when President Kennedy announced that the United States had discovered through aerial reconnaissance the presence of Soviet intermediate-range ballistic missiles and jet bombers in Cuba. From October 16 to 28, the United States and the Soviet Union were locked in a nuclear confrontation that was resolved only through intense military pressure and diplomatic negotiations. From the outset, the United States insisted that all offensive strategic weapons be withdrawn from Cuba and that the missile sites be dismantled. To convey this position, President Kennedy negotiated directly with Soviet Premier Nikita Khrushchev. Reinforcing this diplomacy, the United States increased its military preparations for war against Cuba, and if necessary, against the Soviet Union. All U.S. military forces throughout the world went to a higher stage of military alert. In 1961, there were five stages of alert (Defense Condition 1 through 5). Most U.S. forces in the crisis went to Defense Condition 3; SAC went to Defense Condition 2. As the crisis deepened, U.S. naval forces in the Atlantic imposed a blockade, or quarantine, on Cuba by sending 90 ships and flying 9,000 naval air sorties over the Soviet ships approaching the island nation. The Strategic Air Command went on continuous airborne alert with 57 B–52s and 61 tankers in the air around the clock. SAC's ICBM force, 90 Atlases and 46 Titans, were brought to a higher state of alert. The command's B–47 fleet was dispersed to preselected civilian and military airfields, thus lessening their vulnerability in any massed enemy attack. For thirteen days President Kennedy and his advisors negotiated with Premier Khrushchev, until on October 27, 1962, the Russian agreed to withdraw the offensive weapons from Cuba. For more than a month afterwards, the U.S. Navy blockaded the island, insuring compliance with the negotiated withdrawal of the offensive missiles and aircraft. See Graham T. Allison, *Essence of Decision: Explaining the Cuban Missile Crisis* (Boston, 1971); Scott D. Sagan, "Nuclear Alerts and Crisis Management," *International Security*

barrel he had ever stared at, once Strategic Air Command did in fact generate its forces.[128] Remember that it all started with proof of the pudding brought back by strategic reconnaissance, continued with strategic surveillance, both of Cuba and the approaches to Cuba by sea. The Russians had no alternative but to step down and do what they were asked to do. End of speech. But I guess the simple point is that even during the Kennedy administration, the value of superiority was so obvious that it couldn't be missed.

Burchinal: It was totally missed by the Kennedy administration, by both the executive leadership and by McNamara. They did not understand what had been created and handed to them, and what it had given them. SAC was about at its peak. We had, not supremacy, but complete nuclear superiority over the Soviets. Fortunately, there was enough panic in Washington when they saw those missiles going in, and it was a new team, of course, with Kennedy and McNamara and company, that they gave only the broadest

---

9 (Spring 1985): 106–122; Marc Trachtenberg, "The Influence of Nuclear Weapons in the Cuban Missile Crisis," and "White House Tapes and Minutes of the Cuban Missile Crisis," *International Security* 10 (Summer 1985): 137–163, 164–203.

[128] Nikita Khrushchev (1894–1971) was a native of Kursk, Russia, who came to power in 1953, following the death of Stalin. For a brief period he shared power with five other Soviet leaders who constituted the Presidium. In early 1954 Khrushchev emerged as the sole leader of the Soviet Union. A powerful, somewhat eccentric leader, he changed the direction of Soviet history in 1956 in a secret speech to the 20th Party Congress in which he denounced the excesses of Stalin's one-man rule and repudiated the concept that Soviet Communism was the single, infallible authority in the communist world. In the same speech he outlined a new Soviet foreign policy of "peaceful coexistence" with the western nations. Unlike Stalin, Khrushchev traveled extensively in the West, including the United States, visiting with President Eisenhower and other American officials in 1959. A dominating, often crude figure, he attended a session of the United Nations General Assembly in New York and when a speaker made some anti-Soviet remarks, the Soviet leader shouted back obscenities, pounded his fists, and removed his shoe, banging it repeatedly on the desk. In 1961, when Khrushchev met with the then newly elected President Kennedy in Vienna, Austria, Khrushchev perceived that Kennedy would be a weak president. Shortly thereafter Khrushchev moved to change the postwar status of Berlin. In a speech to the Soviet military in June 1961, he outlined his plans for unilaterally removing Berlin from control of the United States, France, Great Britain, and the Soviet Union, making it a free city in the midst of East Germany, a satellite state of the Soviet Union. In August, East Germany moved to stop the flood of refugees into West Berlin by constructing a wall. In this crisis, American military forces were mobilized and sent to Germany. The Cuban Missile Crisis of October 1962, perhaps the most serious confrontation ever between the United States and the Soviet Union, thus capped three years of heightened tensions between the two nations, tensions which also included conflict and competition in Latin America and the Far East as well as Europe and the Caribbean. For biographies of Khrushchev see Edward Crankshaw, *Khrushchev: A Career* (New York, 1967); Roy A. Medvedev and Zhores A. Medvedev, *Khrushchev: The Years in Power* (New York, 1976). For accounts of Khrushchev and the Cuban Missile Crisis see Robert M. Slusser, *The Berlin Crisis of 1961* (Baltimore, 1973); Arnold L. Horelick, "The Cuban Missile Crisis, An Analysis of Soviet Calculations and Behavior," *World Politics* 16 (April 1964): 363–389.

indication of what they wanted in terms of support for the President. So we were able at the military level, from the JCS on down (without involving the politicians) to put SAC on a one-third airborne alert, to disperse part of the force to civilian airfields, with nuclear weapons, to arm our air defense fighter forces with nuclear weapons and disperse them, and to take all of the ICBMs we had, including those still in the contractors' hands, and count them down. These were things that would be visible to the Soviets, just in the event that the tough talk would excite the Soviets sufficiently to think they might want to do something. I remember our Ambassador in Moscow at the time was Foy Kohler.[129] He came back after the Cuban Missile Crisis ended and said that we walked Khrushchev up to the brink of nuclear war, he looked over the edge, and had no stomach for it. We could have written our own book at that time, but our politicians did not understand what happens when you have such a degree of superiority as we had, or they simply didn't know how to use it. They were busily engaged in saving face for the Soviets and making concessions, giving up the IRBMs, the Thors and Jupiters deployed overseas—when all we had to do was write our own ticket.[130]

LeMay: We could have gotten not only the missiles out of Cuba, we could have gotten the Communists out of Cuba at that time.

Johnson: You bet we could have.

---

[129] Foy D. Kohler (1908–), a career foreign service officer, was the U.S. Ambassador to the Soviet Union from 1962 to 1966. He was an expert on Berlin issues, and President Kennedy sent him to Moscow to negotiate with Premier Khrushchev on Berlin. See Foy D. Kohler and Mose L. Harvey, eds., *The Soviet Union: Yesterday, Today, and Tomorrow* (Miami, 1975), 122–133.

[130] At the peak of the Cuban Missile Crisis, on October 27, 1962, when a military invasion of Cuba seemed imminent, Attorney General Robert F. Kennedy met with Soviet Ambassador to the United States Anatoly Dobrynin. They discussed conditions for settling the crisis in which the Soviets would yield to the American naval quarantine and remove all offensive strategic weapons from Cuba, while in return, the United States would act to persuade the NATO nations to remove 15 Jupiter missiles from Turkey. These discussions did not produce a formal agreement, but they did result in an "understanding" between key government officials. As the crisis deepened, President Kennedy advocated strongly carrying out the terms of this "understanding." Most of his advisors, however, opposed this course of action, arguing that the United States' overwhelming military strength was sufficient to force Soviet withdrawal from Cuba. In the end, Kennedy overruled them and once the crisis passed, the missiles were removed from Turkey in 1963. The 60 Thor IRBMs in England were not part of the negotiations. Prior to the crisis, the United States had intended to retire the Jupiter missiles because of their inaccuracy and vulnerability to a Soviet first strike. See Barton J. Bernstein, "The Cuban Missile Crisis: Trading the Jupiters in Turkey?" *Political Science Quarterly* 95 (Spring 1980): 97–125; Allison, *Essence of Decision*, 141–142, 225–226; Trachtenberg, "White House Tapes and Minutes of the Cuban Missile Crisis," *International Security* 10 (Summer 1985): 143–146; David A. Welch and James G. Blight, "The Eleventh Hour of the Cuban Missile Crisis: An Introduction to the Excomm Transcripts," *International Security* 12 (1987/88): 5–29; McGeorge Bundy, trans., and James F. Blight, ed., "October 27, 1962: Transcripts of the Meetings of the Excomm," *International Security* 12 (1987/88): 30–92.

LeMay: Let's go back a little further. For a year or so before the Cuban Missile Crisis, there appeared in the newspapers and magazines statements by various people, Congressmen and so forth, that there were missiles in Cuba. The administration would come back and say, "there is no evidence that there are missiles in Cuba." Finally they gave the mission to SAC to overfly Cuba with our U–2s, and they found the missiles.[131] With this Kennedy had to do something because he had been saying all the time that, "No, there aren't any there." So he made a speech over radio. I didn't think it was a very tough speech, but Khrushchev thought it was tough.

I actually saw a message that indicated to me that we could have gotten the Communists out of Cuba. I was at my desk, and Ellis was my exec.[132] He would come in and lift up that pile of papers and shove some more on the bottom every once in a while, and I never got to the bottom. I called him in one day with a paper that I wanted some action on right away. I buzzed him, and he came in, and I gave him instructions on that. When he came in he had another pile of papers on his arm. Instead of putting them in the in-basket underneath, he laid them on the desk. Since I wanted action right quick, he took the paper and took off with a high lope, leaving the papers on the desk. Instead of reaching in the basket, I reached on that pile and got one off, and there was a message from Khrushchev, which indicated to me that we could get the Communists out of Cuba. It wasn't five minutes—I had just gotten through reading this thing when he came in and started shuffling through papers. I said, "What are you looking for? This?" I had a suspicion he was. He said, "Yes. It has been withdrawn; it shouldn't have been circulated." That's the last we saw of that. Instead of ridding Cuba of the Communists, they made a deal that if we took our missiles out of Italy and Turkey they would take theirs out of Cuba.

---

[131] On October 14, 1962, Maj. Richard S. Heyser flew a SAC U–2 reconnaissance aircraft over western Cuba and photographed construction of a Soviet medium-range missile base. Within a day the film had been processed and the sites identified by CIA, State, and Defense Department intelligence experts. This photographic evidence was presented to President Kennedy on the morning of October 16, beginning the United States' actions in the crisis. Two weeks later, Maj. Rudolph Anderson, Jr., a SAC pilot, was killed while flying a special U–2 reconnaissance mission over Cuba. He was awarded the Distinguished Service Medal posthumously. See Hopkins, "Development of the Strategic Air Command," 107–108; Arthur M. Schlesinger, Jr., *A Thousand Days: John F. Kennedy in the White House* (Boston, 1965), 799–835.

[132] Gen. Richard H. Ellis (1919–), a native of Delaware, graduated from Dickinson College in Carlisle, Pennsylvania, in 1941. Following Pearl Harbor, he joined the Army Air Forces, serving in the Pacific. In 1944, Ellis became a colonel at age 25, one of the youngest in the Army Air Forces. After the war he returned to school, completing a law degree. During the Korean War he was recalled to active duty, serving as an operations planner in the United States and Europe. When that war ended, Colonel Ellis remained in the Air Force, holding a succession of staff and command positions. From 1961 to 1963 he was General LeMay's executive officer at Headquarters, USAF. Later, in the 1970s, he served as Director of Plans at Headquarters Air Force, commanded all USAF forces in Europe (1975–77), and commanded the Strategic Air Command (1977–81).

U–2 reconnaissance aircraft.

Later I got a little plaque with the month on there and in black, "The 10-day Period of the Cuban Missile Crisis," with a little note from the President thanking us for our support during this very critical time. During that very critical time, in my mind there wasn't a chance that we would have gone to war with Russia because we had overwhelming strategic capability and the Russians knew it.

Burchinal: And we made it visible to them.

Catton: Let me add just an underline to that because I think it is so important that we understand the versatility and flexibility of long-range air. During the Cuban Missile Crisis, who found the missiles? U–2s from SAC: long-range air. Then the strategic forces were generated up to about eighty percent, meaning that we had ready for launch perhaps four out of five of our bombers and tankers in SAC. And a portion of that eighty percent was on airborne alert.

Burchinal: Those were ten days when neither Curt nor I went home. We slept in the Pentagon right around the clock, beginning before the President's

116

Soviet missile equipment photographed in Cuba.

announcement that produced the crisis.[133] Along the way, after we had assumed our alert posture, one of our U–2s out of Alaska had a malfunction in his navigation system and wound up over the Chukotski Peninsula.[134] We knew the Soviet radar was following him. I remember word came to the

---

[133] LeMay and Burchinal were, respectively, Chief of Staff, USAF, and Deputy Chief of Staff for Plans and Operations, Headquarters, USAF. Thus, General LeMay represented the Air Force on the Joint Chiefs of Staff, and Lt. Gen. Burchinal was LeMay's deputy for operations. Burchinal was responsible for developing and coordinating Air Force plans and for overseeing operations. He represented the Air Force and General LeMay at JCS meetings when the principals of the military services were not present.

[134] The Chukotski Peninsula is a small jut of land near the Bering Sea. It is the most eastern part of the Soviet Union, and the United States flew regular reconnaissance flights along the Pacific rim observing activities on the peninsula. This U–2 incident occurred on Saturday, October 27, 1962, when a SAC reconnaissance aircraft inadvertently flew over Soviet territory. Although this U–2 incident was unrelated to the Cuban Missile Crisis, the perception that there was a linkage on the part of the Soviets was possible. The Soviets did not react militarily to the SAC U–2 aircraft flying over Chukotski, although Premier Khrushchev did write President Kennedy on October 28th expressing his displeasure and noting that at a key moment in the crisis the "intruding American plane could be easily taken for a nuclear bomber." Kennedy responded and explained the accidental and coincidental nature of the Pacific U–2 episode, and pledged to avoid a recurrence in the future. See Sagan, "Nuclear Alerts and Crisis Management," *International Security* 9 (Spring 1985): 118–120; Roger Hilsman, *To Move A Nation* (Garden City, N.Y., 1967), 221.

Gen. Curtis LeMay presents Distinguished Service Medal to Lt. Gen. David A. Burchinal.

tank,[135] and McNamara was with the JCS. He left us in a great state of agitation to go get the President on the phone to apologize to the Russians. The JCS said, "No. Tell them, don't touch that thing, or they've had it." The Russians knew what was going on anyway, because our controllers in Alaska contacted the aircraft on the radio, gave him his correct course, and got him back out of there. There was no reaction on the Soviets' part, because they were stood down.

Kohn: Perhaps the Cuban Missile Crisis confirms part of what Douhet and others were saying in the 1920s: strategic air power can decide the great issues of peace and war.

Burchinal: It was a unique situation that very rarely occurs. We had such total superiority at that time that there was no question, no contest. As the

---

[135] The "tank" is the meeting room for the Joint Chiefs of Staff. Customarily, the chairman, the vice chairman (added in 1987), and the service chiefs—Army, Navy, Air Force, and Marine Corps—meet on a regular basis. During periods of crises, meetings in the "tank" are often continuous. See Lawrence J. Korb, *The Joint Chiefs of Staff: The First Twenty-Five Years* (Bloomington, Ind., 1976), 21–25.

Russians built up their capacity during the 1960s and into the early 1970s, that situation no longer obtained. It has since always worried me that publications about the Cuban Missile Crisis all claim that we were so close to nuclear war; ninety-nine percent of the people who write about it don't understand the truth.

Kohn: Why do you say that, General Burchinal?

Burchinal: Because the Russians were so thoroughly stood down, and we knew it. They didn't make any move. They did not increase their alert; they did not increase any flights, or their air defense posture. They didn't do a thing, they froze in place. We were never further from nuclear war than at the time of Cuba, never further.

Kohn: In reading some of the literature on the Cuban Missile Crisis, one gets the impression that the civilian leadership of the country was so horrified by the prospect of war in any shape or form that they were really making every effort to draw back at the first opportunity. That's my sense of it, but that's only from the literature. All of you were there and knew the political leadership; you worked with them.

Johnson: They were very good at putting out brave words, but they didn't do a bloody thing to back them up except what, inadvertently, we did.

LeMay: That was the mood prevalent with top civilian leadership; you are quite correct.

The War In Southeast Asia

Kohn: At this time and in the following two years, there must have been some talk of Southeast Asia. Was there any planning going on in 1962, 1963, or 1964 that you remember, or any discussion about how one would use air power in a war like the one we would be facing in Southeast Asia?

LeMay: You mean before we moved into Vietnam at all?

Kohn: Yes, when we were still in the advisory role, slowly building up our advisors during the Kennedy years, the **FARM GATE** operations. We were talking then also about some herbicide operations, but well before we really

119

began to use our air power and to put American units into South Vietnam—before 1965.[136]

Burchinal: We were selling airplanes, ones they could fly, to the Vietnamese, giving them the air capability because we recognized they were going to have to have air capability if they were going to succeed.

Catton: David, don't you remember—you were in the Pentagon a lot earlier than I, and of course, General LeMay was there all of this time—but after Cuba, and in the beginnings of what became the Southeast Asia conflict, I can remember that the administration, particularly McNamara, was vociferous against providing any American-operated military force in the theater, and particularly air.

Burchinal: Oh, yes. That's what I said. We were using *them*—the Vietnamese—selling *them* the airplanes and training *them* to fly them. Our involvement was not overtly in combat at that point, only with our Military Assistance Advisory Group.[137]

---

[136] Until 1961, the United States had a small military advisory group of less than 700 men in South Vietnam. During the Kennedy administration (1961–63), the number of American military advisors in Vietnam increased to 16,263, including 4,600 Air Force personnel. In the first year of the Johnson administration that figure grew to 23,310. The Americanization of the war began in 1965 with the introduction of large units of Army and Marine forces. By the end of 1965, there were 180,000 American military personnel in Vietnam; by January 1969 that figure had grown to 542,000. In the early years code names were used to designate combat forces in Vietnam. FARM GATE was the code name for the first Air Force combat unit, the 4400th Combat Crew Training Squadron, sent to Vietnam in October 1961. The squadron's mission was to train the South Vietnamese air forces in counterinsurgency tactics and to fly combat operations in support of U.S. Army Special Forces and Rangers. See Guenter Lewy, *America in Vietnam* (New York, 1978); Robert F. Futrell, *The United States Air Force in Southeast Asia: The Advisory Years to 1965* (Washington, 1981), 79–84, 127–134, 136–146, 157–159; Stanley Karnow, *Vietnam: A History* (New York, 1983), 206–240.

[137] American Military Assistance Advisory Group (MAAG) went to Saigon, South Vietnam, in 1950 with 65 officers and men. With few exceptions this was an Army group, and its mission was administrative: to assist the French military in Indo-China in requisitioning, procuring, and receiving American supplies and equipment. After the Geneva Conference of 1954 and the French withdrawal, the American MAAG remained in Saigon, although its mission was altered to include training of the South Vietnamese forces. Led by Lt. Gen. Samuel T. Williams, U.S. Army, the size of the group fluctuated between 600 and 700 men drawn from all of the military services. The Army continued its predominance in people and mission, although there were a few Air Force officers and men there to train pilots in the small 3,000-man South Vietnamese Air Force. From 1961 until the Americanization of the war in 1965, the size of the MAAG gradually expanded, and its mission changed in two fundamental ways: first, the administrative burden of distributing and accounting for U.S. aid increased dramatically; second, the advisors' direct combat support to the South Vietnamese forces became routine. In January 1962, the MAAG in Saigon became the Military Assistance Command, Vietnam (MAC–V), the principal American military command that conducted the war. Ronald H. Spector, *United States Army in Vietnam, Advice and Support: The Early Years* (Washington, 1983), 115–121, 259–262; Futrell, *Advisory Years*, 46–59, 79–84; Lewy, *America in Vietnam*, 22–24.

Catton: We might even go back to flexible response for just a moment. Everybody can define a phrase, but we witnessed what some people thought was flexible response. The administration and the civilian leadership in the Pentagon determined that flexible response was "use just enough, *not too much.*" Flexible response in that manner was and is absolutely a loser. We always were forced to use just enough military power to get the job done and no more. Of course, when you use that philosophy, you always come out a loser. That happened and was going on during the standdown of Cuba and certainly was reflected in the efforts over there in Vietnam throughout, but particularly before 1965 and 1966.

Burchinal: Remember these were the Whiz Kids, the so-called intellectuals, who thought they had all the answers.[138] They didn't understand military power, and particularly, they did not understand air power. They thought they could use it like a scalpel in a bloody hospital operation, where as in truth military force is a pretty damn blunt instrument. You use it for maximum shock effect—hard, fast, and continuous—and get the job done. They wanted to use it to just cut a little here, and cut a little there, and sew that one up, and cut a little more over here. That was their whole philosophy on using air power in Vietnam. And of course, that was a bloody disaster.

Catton: General LeMay, did you have to fight those guys all the time to get them to give us some authority and some capability to use air over there?

LeMay: Constantly, constantly. To start off with on this flexible response business, I think that phrase is an outgrowth to counter the "immorality" of the massive retaliation that everybody thought meant we would dump all the atomic weapons we had automatically on a poor helpless foe. That was immoral; flexible response was, "No, we don't have to do that. We are just going to use what force is necessary to do the job." Of course, this violates the principles of war, and over the centuries we have found that it doesn't work.

---

[138] When Robert McNamara became Secretary of Defense in 1961, he assembled on his staff a small group of experts drawn from various fields who became known, by critics and admirers alike, as the "Whiz Kids." Along with McNamara, they dominated formulation of defense policy and decisionmaking in the Defense Department for the next eight years. The most prominent of these men were Alain G. Enthoven, Charles J. Hitch, K. Wayne Smith, Henry Rowen, Russell Murray, Adam Yarmolinsky, and Daniel Ellsberg. Led by Hitch and Enthoven, these civilian advisers used systems analysis and economics to devise and implement a new planning-programming-budgeting system (PPBS). That system forced the military services to bring their operational plans and weapons programs into alignment with their annual budget requests. In turn, this system allowed McNamara and his advisors to choose between service programs and to set priorities. See Alain C. Enthoven and K. Wayne Smith, *How Much Is Enough? Shaping the Defense Program 1961–1969* (New York, 1971); Charles J. Hitch, *Decision-making for Defense* (New York, 1965); Kaufman, *McNamara Strategy.*

Maj. Gen. Ton That Dinh, Commander of II Army Corps of Armed Forces for Republic of Vietnam, explains the usage of the native bow gun to Gen. Curtis LeMay, Chief of Staff, USAF, during LeMay's trip to Vietnam in April 1962.

But we couldn't convince anybody in the Pentagon at the time it wouldn't work.

Burchinal: It also conveyed to the enemy a clear impression of weakness, of lack of will. You don't have the will, really, or the guts, when push comes to shove.

LeMay: That's right. And they were right; we didn't have it.

Burchinal: Exactly; we didn't have it at the political level. By the way, Dick, don't ever use "counterforce targeting" and "McNamara" in the same paragraph. He gutted any capability we had for counterforce targeting. He would absolutely not let us program forces for counterforce targeting. I once took him a program when the Soviets had started to build up a pretty reasonable intercontinental missile force. I wanted on the basis of our missile PK and reliability factors to buy enough Minutemen to put reliably one missile on every bloody silo he had—just one.[139] He wouldn't have any part

---

[139] PK stands for probability of kill. It is a term used in operational planning which indicates numerically the probability of a weapon destroying a target. Minuteman missiles were the United States' principal land-based, intercontinental ballistic missiles from the Kennedy administration (1961–63) to the present. By 1964, the Air Force had 700 Minuteman I missiles assigned to the Strategic Air Command. During the next ten years, the total number of operational Minuteman missiles, positioned in hardened, underground silos and continuously ready to be launched, grew to 1,000. However, by 1969, newer models, the Minuteman II and III, had replaced the first generation of missiles. John W.R. Taylor, ed., *Jane's All the World's Aircraft, 1969–1970* (London, 1970), 583–584.

of it. He was the one that forced us into this sort of assured destruction, minimum deterrence level, where it did almost force us to put cities and civilian populations at some risk, as hostage, because we didn't have enough force to do a proper military job.

LeMay: To get back to your question, "Was there any planning for the use of the air power in Vietnam?" There was some after we got fully embroiled over there. As a matter of fact, we got ground forces involved in there before I knew anything about it, but I don't remember any discussion where we would use our ground forces in Asia until it was right there, happening. The decision was made and there we were, involved. The Joint Chiefs finally came up with a target list of ninety targets in North Vietnam, targets that would badly reduce the North Vietnamese capability of supporting the war in the South. But it was never approved, and we were never given authority to get them.[140]

Kohn: Was that after we began Rolling Thunder?[141]

Burchinal: No. Rolling Thunder was substantially later.

Johnson: It seemed to me that the handwriting was on the wall quite a bit earlier over there. Think back to Korea. I remember that Eisenhower promised that if elected, he would go to Korea. He went and got about the same settlement that Truman could have had any time he wanted it. We left our troops over there, and they are still there. Looking at that in 1961, I know

---

[140] On November 1, 1964, the Joint Chiefs of Staff verbally recommended to Secretary McNamara that the Air Force commence within sixty to seventy-two hours the systematic bombing of ninety-four strategic targets in North Vietnam. When President Johnson considered this recommendation, both Secretary of Defense McNamara and Secretary of State Dean Rusk advised a policy of restraint. Consequently, the President decided not to launch the air strikes; instead he opted for a much more restrained and limited air campaign called BARREL ROLL. See Futrell, *The Advisory Years to 1965*, 253–256.

[141] ROLLING THUNDER was the code name for the expanded, intermittent air campaign by American air forces against North Vietnam from February 1965 to March 1968. Its purpose was to strike at North Vietnam and persuade that government to seek a negotiated peace. Two other objectives were to use American air power to boost South Vietnamese morale and to demonstrate United States resolve following the destruction by the Viet Cong of a U.S. Army barracks which killed 23 soldiers. During ROLLING THUNDER Air Force and Navy forces flew 306,380 sorties and dropped 640,000 tons of bombs on North Vietnam. See Lewy, *America in Vietnam*, 375–406; William W. Momyer, *Airpower in Three Wars* (Washington, 1978), 90–98; Carl Berger, ed., *United States Air Force in Southeast Asia, 1961–1973: An Illustrated Account* (Washington, 1977), 74–89; U.S. Grant Sharp, *Strategy For Defeat: Vietnam in Retrospect* (San Rafael, Calif., 1978), 94–104; James Clay Thompson, *Rolling Thunder, Understanding Policy and Program Failure* (Chapel Hill, 1980); John Morrocco, *Thunder From Above: Air War 1941–1968* (Boston, 1984), 50–71; U.S. Department of Defense, *The Pentagon Papers: The Senator Gravel Edition*, 4 vols., (Boston, 1972), III, 284–286, 321–324, 332–334, 339–340, IV, 55–56, 68–70, 109–110, 138, 421–422.

that I thought we had no business going into a situation where we were going to repeat what we had done in Korea. When I retired in 1961, and was called back to active duty, I went over to see McGeorge Bundy and pleaded with him not to get us involved, to supply the South Vietnamese all we could, but not make it our war.[142] I went with the same thing to Max Taylor,[143] who was advising Kennedy, and I went to Lemnitzer.[144] All of them were very polite

---

[142] McGeorge Bundy (1919–) was the Special Assistant to the President for National Security Affairs in the Kennedy and Johnson administrations. A New Englander, Bundy was a brilliant student at Yale (1940) and Harvard where he was a junior fellow. Following military service in World War II, he helped research and write the autobiography of Secretary of War Henry L. Stimson. In 1949 he joined the faculty at Harvard, rising in five years to become professor of government and subsequently, Dean of the faculty of Arts and Sciences. When John F. Kennedy was elected President in 1960, he asked Bundy to be his special assistant. As such, Bundy helped shape American military policy in both the Kennedy and Johnson administrations. In 1966 he resigned, becoming the president of the Ford Foundation. See Joseph Kraft, *Profiles in Power* (New York, 1966), 163–175; David Halberstam, *The Best and the Brightest* (New York, 1972), 40–63.

[143] Gen. Maxwell D. Taylor (1901–87) was a professional soldier who graduated from West Point in 1922. A brilliant student and leader, he went into the Field Artillery but returned to the academy to teach on two occasions in the interwar years. In July 1941, he joined the staff of Gen. George C. Marshall, Army Chief of Staff. In World War II Taylor served as Chief of Staff of the 82d Airborne Division, and later Commander of the 101st Airborne Division. He led that division in the Normandy Invasion, parachuting behind Utah Beach and capturing key causeways leading from the beaches to the interior areas. Following the war, he rose in the Army, becoming Superintendent of West Point (1946–49); Commander, U.S. Eighth Army in Korea (1953); and Chief of Staff, U.S. Army (1955–59). He retired in 1959 and wrote a successful book, *The Uncertain Trumpet* (1959), which criticized the Eisenhower administration's military policy of massive retaliation and advocated a new policy of flexible response. Then in an unprecented action, General Taylor came out of retirement to become President Kennedy's Military Representative to the President. He served for two years in the White House, then President Kennedy selected him to be Chairman of the Joint Chiefs of Staff. He led the JCS from 1962–64. For perspective on General Taylor's service to President Kennedy see Duan Van Lee, "From the New Look to Flexible Response," and B. Franklin Cooling, "The Vietnam War, 1962–1973," in Kenneth J. Hagan and William R. Roberts, eds., *Against All Enemies: Interpretations of American Military History from Colonial Times to the Present* (New York, 1986), 321–340, 341–360; Russell F. Weigley, *The American Way of War: A History of United States Military Strategy and Policy* (Bloomington, Ind., 1973), 441–477.

[144] Gen. Lyman L. Lemnitzer (1899–), U.S. Army, was the Chairman of the Joint Chiefs of Staff during the first two years of the Kennedy administration (1961–63). Lemnitzer graduated from West Point in 1920 and entered the Artillery Branch. He served in the Philippine Islands, Fort Monroe, (Virginia), and West Point before World War II. A specialist in military planning, Lemnitzer worked for Gen. George C. Marshall, Army Chief of Staff, in 1940–41 as the Army began mobilizing and equipping the nation's ground and air forces for war. During the war Lemnitzer served on Lt. Gen. Dwight D. Eisenhower's staff in planning and carrying out the Allied invasion of North Africa. In 1943 he became the Chief of Staff to Field Marshal Harold R.L.G. Alexander, Supreme Allied Commander, Mediterranean. From that point forward and for the remainder of his professional career, Lemnitzer was associated with planning and leading Allied forces. After the war he was selected by Secretary of Defense James Forrestal to be the American military officer responsible for planning and establishing the North Atlantic Treaty Organization's military forces. In the 1950s, General Lemnitzer rose to become the Vice Chief, then Chief of Staff of the Army (1957–60). After serving as Chairman of the Joint Chiefs of Staff

except Lemnitzer, and he was very rude. I couldn't see how we would ever get out. That was what was troubling me all the time, because we knew we were going to be under control, as we were in Korea.

Kohn: What do you mean by "you knew you would be under control," General Johnson?

Johnson: I meant that we would be limited as to what military actions we could take.

Kohn: So you believed that, from the beginning, we would never be able to work our will?

Johnson: I couldn't see how we could get out of there without leaving another division or two there the rest of my life.

Kohn: Did you think from the beginning that we would not be permitted to wage a strategic campaign against North Vietnam as we had done in World War II?

Johnson: We were very limited in Korea, so I believed the civilians would impose the same limitations and the same problem.

Burchinal: Curt, was there ever a time during Vietnam when the recommendation was made that we go up and burn down North Vietnam?

LeMay: Yes. When we finally got that target list through the Joint Chiefs.

Burchinal: Because that would have ended the war real quick, just like it did in Japan.

LeMay: We could have ended it in any ten-day period you wanted to, but they never would bomb the target list we had.

Burchinal: We could have dropped circulars like we did in Japan and said, "Get out because this town won't be here tomorrow."

Kohn: Do you all think that what we did in the Southeast Asia war was at all a strategic air campaign, as you learned to wage strategic air war in your military careers?

(1960–62), he went to Europe, becoming the Supreme Allied Commander, Europe. In July 1969 General Lemnitzer retired, having served the nation as a soldier for 49 years.

LeMay: Definitely not. It wasn't until the last two weeks of the war that we even approached it. When we turned the B–52s loose up north—that started what would have been a strategic campaign, and it would have been completely over in a few more days if we had just continued it.[145] A few more days' work and we would have been completely free without any casualties because all of the SAMs [surface-to-air missiles] were gone by that time. Their bases and warehouses supplying the SAM sites were gone, too. So it would have been a pretty free ride from then on, and we would have completely won the war. Up until that time, even when we were using the B–52s, we were bombing jungle because there was a rumor there might be some Viet Cong in that jungle. So they would give us a point in the jungle, and we would go hit it.

B–52 stratofortresses bomb enemy concentrations along the Ho Chi Minh Trail.

---

[145] In the final weeks of the war, President Nixon ordered a bombing campaign against North Vietnam. Nixon acted because North Vietnam had suspended on December 13, 1972, diplomatic negotiations on a cease-fire agreement ending the fighting and returning U.S. prisoners of war. The bombing campaign, known as Operation Linebacker II, began on December 18 and lasted for 11 days. Air Force B–52s flew 729 sorties, and Navy and Air Force fighter-bombers flew approximately 1,000 sorties. A total of 20,370 tons of bombs were dropped on North Vietnam, damaging military and civilian structures, electrical power networks, petroleum storage depots, railroad yards and tracks, and antiaircraft defenses. On December 29 the bombing stopped; North Vietnam agreed to resume negotiations. Three weeks later, on January 23, 1973, the final cease-fire agreement was signed by Henry Kissinger for the United States and Le Duc Tho for North Vietnam. See James R. McCarthy and George B. Allison, *Linebacker II: A View From the Rock* (Montgomery, Ala., 1979), 39–89, 91–167; Berger, ed., *The United States Air Force in Southeast Asia*, 95–99; Richard M. Nixon, *RN, The Memoirs of Richard Nixon* (New York, 1978), 717–744; Henry Kissinger, *White House Years* (Boston, 1979), 717–744; W. Hays Park, "Linebacker and the Law of War," *Air University Review* 34 (Jan-Feb 1983): 2–30.

Burchinal: An area 100-yards wide or 1,000-yards wide by thousands of yards long, and there we would go and dump bombs in that area.[146]

Kohn: Instead of having a target that made sense to end the war or to undermine the enemy's military capability?

LeMay: Yes.

Catton: I guess you could also say that the Arc Light sorties, in the Arc Light campaigns, were in direct support of ground troops; the use of strategic assets in a tactical mode.[147]

Burchinal: There is one thing, which bears on what General LeMay said. "Johnny" Vogt,[148] who was there and very close to it, insists that at the time

---

[146] A typical formation of B–52Ds was three aircraft, each capable of dropping a maximum of 108 500-pound bombs (approximately 54,000 pounds). Normally, B–52s deployed with a mix of 500- and 750-pound bombs, mounted externally and internally. Together a cell of three bombers could cover an area of a mile-and-a-half long and a half-mile wide.

[147] In the spring of 1965 Gen. William Westmoreland, Commander of the U.S. Military Assistance Command, Vietnam, requested that air power interdict the movement of enemy troops and supplies in the jungles of Vietnam and Laos. He received the authority, and in June 1965 B–52s from the Strategic Air Command began flying from bases in Guam to Southeast Asia where they dropped 500- and 750-pound conventional, high-explosive bombs on supply trails, depots, and suspected troop concentrations in the Vietnamese jungles. ARC LIGHT was the code name for these B–52 operations. General Westmoreland in his memoirs characterized the B–52 as "the weapon the enemy feared most" and "the most lethal weapon employed in Vietnam." Between June 1965 and August 1973, SAC B–52s flew 126,615 sorties, losing 18 aircraft to hostile fire. For an overview see Berger, ed., *The USAF in Southeast Asia*, 149–167; William C. Westmoreland, *A Soldier Reports* (New York, 1976), 137–138, 418, 283, 340; Lewy, *America in Vietnam*, 374–417; and Morrocco, *Thunder From Above, The Air War 1941–1968*, 86–87.

[148] Gen. John S. Vogt (1920–) commanded the Seventh Air Force, the principal USAF air force in South Vietnam, from April 1972 to August 1973. A first generation military officer, Vogt was a fighter pilot and ace in World War II. He rose to command a squadron, participating in every major tactical air campaign in northern Europe in 1944–45. He left the service in 1946, enrolled in Yale University, and upon graduation he reentered the Air Force in 1949. He progressed quickly in the officer corps, holding key junior staff assignments in the National Security Council, Office of the Secretary of Defense, and Joint Chiefs of Staff. Twice he went to the Pacific, first in 1955 as an operations planner, then in 1965 as the Deputy Chief of Staff for Plans and Operations, Pacific Air Forces. In 1968 he became Director of Operations on the Joint Staff. Then in April 1972, General Vogt went to South Vietnam as Commander, Seventh Air Force. The following year the United States signed a cease-fire agreement, and U.S. combat operations ceased. General Vogt left Saigon for Hawaii, assuming command of Pacific Air Forces. Just ten months later he left the Pacific for Europe, assuming command of U.S. Air Forces, Europe. In September 1975, he retired from active duty. For some of Vogt's observations on the air war, see Richard H. Kohn and Joseph P. Harahan, eds., *Air Interdiction in World War II, Korea, and Vietnam: An Interview with Gen. Earle E. Partridge, Gen. Jacob E. Smart, and Gen. John W. Vogt, Jr.* (Washington, 1986), 56–86.

127

Kissinger[149] and the North Vietnamese reached their truce agreement in Paris we had, in effect, won the war. The North Vietnamese had had enough. We were going to move our air force that was in Vietnam back to Thailand, and keep our total air capability in place. The minute we didn't, of course, North Vietnam moved right in and took over. And we didn't have the will to follow through on the plan which Kissinger had negotiated.

Catton: Actually the Congress prevented it, David.[150]

Burchinal: Yes, that's right. There was no will left anywhere in the government to continue a major military force in that theater.

Catton: Dick, let me back up one. General LeMay, how would you characterize the similarity between Linebacker II and the plan that we took to the government, took to the Secretary of Defense and the White House, back in 1964–65?[151]

LeMay: The first plan we had was 90 strategic targets, and I don't know what the target objective was in Linebacker II.

Catton: The targets, of course, would be a little bit different in detail, but the philosophy, the concept of the operation, to my mind was very similar.

LeMay: In that we stopped bombing jungles and started getting more important targets.

---

[149] Henry A. Kissinger (1923–) was the Assistant to the President for National Security during the Nixon administration. As such, he was the principal negotiator with the North Vietnamese in Paris from 1969 to 1973. For an account of the negotiations see Kissinger, *White House Years*, 717–744; Marvin Kalb and Bernard Kalb, *Kissinger* (New York, 1974), 336–422; Gareth Porter, *A Peace Denied: The United States, Vietnam, and the Paris Agreement* (Bloomington, Ind., 1975), 13–206.

[150] In April 1972, Senators Frank Church (Idaho) and Clifford Case (New Jersey) amended an appropriations bill funding the Department of State to direct the cutoff of all funds for United States combat operations in Southeast Asia after December 31, 1972, provided a cease-fire agreement included the release of all American prisoners of war. Although this Church-Case Amendment was weakened in the Senate, it became law in the summer of 1972. In addition, there were other laws enacted which placed limitations on U.S. military actions in Vietnam. In November 1973, Congress enacted the War Powers Resolution, which limited to 90 days the President's ability to send U.S. forces into combat without receiving congressional approval. This resolution culminated years of growing Congressional resistance to the war which, all told, prevented the United States from coming to the rescue of South Vietnam when it was invaded. U.S. military aid to South Vietnam dropped from $2.2 billion in 1973 to $700 million in 1975, the year that North Vietnam invaded and conquered South Vietnam. See Lewy, *America in Vietnam*, 202–222; John H. Sullivan, *The War Powers Resolution* (Washington, 1982), 31–42, 103–166, 179–184.

[151] For a brief description of the 1965 plan and Linebacker II, see Note 140 and 145.

Catton: It has always been my thought, General LeMay, that if we had been able to go get those 90 targets—and we certainly would have succeeded—we would have saved tens of thousands of lives and many, many years and billions of dollars in that effort. I think we could have made the point way back in 1964–65 by taking on those 90 targets and destroying them.

LeMay: Well, I spent a lot of time trying to bring out the point that in any two-week period or so, we could have, with the proper application of air and naval power, won the war over there.

Catton: That's the point I was hoping you would make.

Burchinal: We should have gone incendiary like we did in Japan: warned them to get out of the way, and then destroyed their means to exist. It wouldn't have cost anything in the way of casualties, really.

LeMay: I want to point out that if you look at the tonnage figures, at the tonnage of bombs that we dropped in the Vietnamese affair, and compare it with what we dropped on Japan and what we dropped on Germany, you will find that we dropped more on Vietnam than we did on Germany and Japan combined.[152] Look what happened to Germany, and above all, look what happened to Japan. There was no invasion necessary there. The only conclusion you can draw is that we were bombing the wrong things in Vietnam.

Kohn: Perhaps you are saying that in the end, the ultimate target is the will of the enemy. It is something Douhet raised back in the 1920s: that you destroy enough or so much that your enemy simply ceases to make war against you.

Burchinal: Destroy the will *and* capability; separate the two.

---

[152] The Comparative U.S. bomb tonnage for World War II, Korea, and Vietnam was as follows:

World War II		
European Theater	2,700,000	tons
Pacific Theater	650,000	tons
Korean War	678,000	tons
Vietnam War	6,162,000	tons

Source: *U.S. Strategic Bombing Survey, Over-all Report (European War)*, September 30, 1945, vol 1, 2; *Summary Report (Pacific War)*, July 1, 1946, vol 1, 16; Futrell, *USAF in Korea, 1950–53*, 689; Report by Directorate of Management Analysis, Headquarters USAF, USAF Management Summary Southeast Asia, September 28, 1973, p 18.

Catton: You have got the right words, Dave.

LeMay: If you destroy their *capability* to win war, then the will to wage war disappears also.

Leadership

Kohn: Could I ask you one last question, about leadership? The issue, General LeMay, is your legendary leadership. Could you reflect on that a bit, what you were trying to do and how you motivated people throughout your career, how you got the job done in your various commands?

LeMay: I don't think we can cover that thoroughly in a short conversation. The main thing is having the right sense of responsibility, trying to get a job done, and transfering that to your troops. It is a team effort, of course, so you have got to get some good working members on your team on the top side, get your plans going, keep the troops abreast of what your goals are, and the way you are going to get it done. Make sure that they feel they can participate in the planning. Make them feel that they are a part of the team and that their thoughts get right up to the top before the decision is made. Once the decision is made, "This is the way we do it," everybody turns to and gets it done. That is the secret to the whole capitalistic system, a system of reward and punishment. If you do the job, you get rewarded. If you didn't get it done, you get fired. Somebody else comes in that will get it done. Of course, in war you have to be kind of ruthless in that regard. Everybody understands that, and they do their best to get the best effort.

Burchinal: Dick, since I worked for Curt about as long as anybody—during the war, in SAC, and in the Pentagon—there are some things he won't say. But I was an observer of his effectiveness, and I will add to what he says because he is probably too modest to tell you about it.

It starts with a thorough knowledge of your own equipment, and the capability of your crews—their training, and their general and specific capabilities. With that very firmly and clearly in mind, in detail, then you need a thorough knowledge of what the enemy can do, either to counter what you are trying to do, or oppose your forces with any degree of success—at least with sufficient effectiveness to stop your particular efforts. You have to have the ability to inspire belief among your troops; that is, they must believe in their mission and in their leader—a mystique, really, rather than charisma. The gentleman we are talking about has that above all else. Decisiveness. You make decisions, and you take the responsibility for them, and nobody questions. Setting an example by your own dedication and work and

130

knowledge seven days a week, twenty-four hours a day, and there is no question in anybody's mind that the service comes first. There is no competition for your loyalty and your dedication, none whatsoever when someone like Curt LeMay is your commander.

Catton: That is very well put, David Burchinal. I agree with what you said. I would add to that, but you know that knowledge and understanding of capabilities and limitations of equipment and people is *so* important. That only comes from dedication, experience, and participation. And of course, you can't do those things unless you are a courageous guy with absolute integrity and dedication. I use the term image instead of mystique, but I like mystique better.

Burchinal: But it is not necessarily charisma.

Catton: I scratched out charisma, Dave.

Kohn: Gentlemen, I greatly appreciate your time and effort in these interviews. Discussing the leadership of General LeMay is a fine way to end the interview.

Johnson: Let me cut in here. I say that the people in the units want to look up to their leaders. They are very anxious to look up to their leaders. If they see that their leaders are trying, are honest and knowledgeable—I won't repeat all the words of Generals Catton and Burchinal because I agree with all of them. But people will follow their leaders if they see the leaders are trying to do the right thing.

Kohn: Thank you all again for sharing your thinking and experiences with the Air Force.

Bibliography

Oral Histories

The United States Air Force Historical Research Center at Maxwell Air Force Base, Alabama, maintains an extensive oral history collection. The following transcribed oral histories were used in preparation for this interview.

Interview, Gen. David A. Burchinal, April 11, 1970
Interview, Gen. Jack J. Catton, July 19–20, 1977
Interview, Gen. Leon W. Johnson, August 26–27, 1975
Interviews, Gen. Curtis E. LeMay, March 11, 1965; January 1965; March 9, 1971; March 29, 1972; and June 8, 1972

Published Sources

Allison, Graham T. *Essence of Decision: Explaining the Cuban Missile Crisis.* Boston: Little, Brown and Company, 1971.
Alperowitz, Gar. *Atomic Diplomacy: Hiroshima and Potsdam.* New York: Simon and Schuster, 1965.
An, Tai Sung. *North Korea: A Political Handbook.* Wilmington, Del.: Scholarly Resources, Inc., 1983.
Anders, Roger M., ed. *Forging the Atomic Shield: Excerpts from the Diary of Gordon E. Dean.* Chapel Hill, N.C.: University of North Carolina Press, 1987.
Appleman, Roy E., and James M. Burns, *et al. Okinawa: The Last Battle.* [U.S. Army in World War II]. Washington: Historical Division, Department of the Army, 1948.
Arnold, Henry H. *Global Mission.* New York: Harper Brothers, Inc., 1949.
Beard, Edmund. *Developing the ICBM, A Study in Bureacratic Politics.* New York: Columbia University Press, 1976.
Berger, Carl, ed. *United States Air Force in Southeast Asia, 1961–1973: An Illustrated Account.* Washington: Office of Air Force History, 1977; rev. ed., 1984.
Bernstein, Barton J. "The Cuban Missile Crisis: Trading the Jupiters in Turkey?" *Political Science Quarterly* 95 (Spring 1980): 97–125.
_____. *Hiroshima and Nagasaki Reconsidered: The Atomic Bombings of Japan and the Origins of the Cold War.* Morristown, N.J.: General Learning Press, 1975.
Blair, Bruce G. *Strategic Command and Control: Reassessing the Nuclear Threat.* Washington: The Brookings Institution, 1985.
Borowski, Harry R. *A Hollow Threat: Strategic Air Power and Containment Before Korea.* Westport, Conn: Greenwood Press, 1982.
Bowers, Peter M. *Boeing Aircraft Since 1916.* New York: Funk and Wagnalls, 1968.

BIBLIOGRAPHY

Boyne, Walter J. *Messerschmitt ME 262: Arrow to the Future*. Washington: Smithsonian Institute Press, 1982.

Bracken, Paul. *The Command and Control of Nuclear Forces*. New Haven: Yale University Press, 1983.

Bundy, McGeorge, trans., and James F. Blight, ed. "October 27, 1962: Transcripts of the Meetings of the Excomm," *International Security* 12 (1987/88): 30–92.

Butow, Robert J. C.. *Japan's Decision to Surrender*. Stanford: Stanford University Press, 1954.

Carson, Kit C., and Robert Mueller. *Combat Chronology 1941–1945*. [The Army Air Forces in World War II]. Washington: Office of Air Force History, 1973.

Carver, Sir Michael, ed. *The War Lords: Military Commanders of the Twentieth Century*. Boston: Little, Brown and Company, 1976.

Ch'en, Jerome. *Mao and the Chinese Revolution*. London: Oxford University Press, 1965.

Churchill, Sir Winston S. *Closing the Ring*. [History of the Second World War]. Boston: Houghton Mifflin, 1951.

Clay, Lucius D. *Decision in Germany*. Garden City, N.Y.: Doubleday and Company, 1950.

Cline, Ray S. *Washington Command Post: The Operations Division*. [U.S. Army in World War II: The War Department]. Washington: Office of the Chief of Military History, 1951.

Coakley, Robert W., and Richard M. Leighton. *Global Logistics and Strategy 1943–1945*. [U.S. Army in World War II: The War Department]. Washington: U.S. Army Center of Military History, 1968.

Coffey, Thomas M. *HAP: The Story of the U.S. Air Force and the Man Who Built It: General Henry H. "Hap" Arnold*. New York: Viking Press, 1982.

——————. *Iron Eagle: The Turbulent Life of General Curtis LeMay*. New York: Crown Publishers, 1986.

Copp, Dewitt S. *Forged in Fire: Strategy and Decisions in the Air War Over Europe 1940–1945*. Garden City, N.Y.: Doubleday and Company, 1982.

Crankshaw, Edward. *Khrushchev: A Career*. New York: Viking Press, 1966.

Craven, Wesley, and James L. Cate, eds. *The Army Air Forces in World War II*. 7 Vols. Chicago: University of Chicago Press, 1948–56; reprint, Washington: Office of Air Force History, 1984.

D'Este, Carlo. *Decision in Normandy*. New York: E.P. Dutton, 1983.

Donovan, Robert J. *Tumultuous Years: The Presidency of Harry S Truman 1949–1953*. New York: Norton, 1982.

Douhet, Giulio. *The Command of the Air*. New York: Coward-McCann, Inc., 1942; reprint, Washington: Office of Air Force History, 1983.

Dugan, James, and Carol Stewart. *Ploesti*. New York: Random House, 1962.

Dupuy, R. Ernest, and Trevor N. Depuy. *The Encyclopedia of Military History*. New York: Harper and Row, 1986.

Enthoven, Alain C., and K. Wayne Smith. *How Much Is Enough? Shaping the Defense Program 1961–1969*. New York: Harper and Row, 1971.

Ethell, Jeff, and Joe Christy. *B-52 Stratofortress*. New York: Charles Scribner and Sons, 1981.

Etzhold, Thomas H., and John L. Gaddis. *Containment: Documents on American Policy and Strategy, 1945–1950*. New York: Columbia University Press, 1978.

Finney, Robert T. *History of the Air Corps Tactical School, 1920–1940*. USAF Historical Study No. 100. Maxwell Air Force Base, Ala.: Air University, 1955.

Foot, Rosemary. *The Wrong War: American Foreign Policy and the Dimensions of the Korean Conflict 1950–1953*. Ithaca, N.Y.: Cornell University Press, 1985.

Frank, Benis M., and Henry I. Shaw, Jr. *Victory and Occupation*. [History of U.S. Marine Corps Operations in World War II]. Washington: Historical Branch, U.S. Marine Corps, 1968.

Frankland, Noble. *The Bombing Offensive Against Germany*. London: Ballentine Press, 1965.

Freedman, Lawrence. *The Evolution of Nuclear Strategy.* New York: St Martin's Press, 1981.

Freeman, Roger. *The Mighty Eighth: A History of the U.S. Eighth Army Air Forces.* Garden City, N.Y.: Doubleday and Company, 1970.

——————. *Mighty Eighth War Diary.* New York: Jane's Publishing, Inc., 1981.

——————. *Mighty Eighth War Manual.* New York: Jane's Publishing, Inc., 1984.

Futrell, Robert T. *Ideas, Concepts, Doctrine: A History of Basic Thinking in the United States Air Force: 1907–1964.* Maxwell Air Force Base, Ala.: Air University Press, 1971.

——————. *The United States Air Force in Korea, 1950–1953.* New York: Duell, Sloan and Pearce, 1961; rev. ed., Washington: Office of Air Force History, 1983.

——————. *The United States Air Force in Southeast Asia: The Advisory Years to 1965.* Washington: Office of Air Force History, 1981.

Gaddis, John L. *Strategies of Containment.* New York: Oxford University Press, 1982.

——————. "The Emerging Post-Revisionist Synthesis on the Origins of the Cold War." *Diplomatic History* 7 (1983): 171–204.

Garand, George W., and Truman R. Strobridge. *Western Pacific Operations.* [History of the U.S. Marine Corps Operations in World War II]. Washington: Historical Branch, U.S. Marine Corps, 1971.

Greenfield, Kent Roberts. *American Strategy in World War II: A Reconsideration.* Baltimore: Johns Hopkins Press, 1963.

——————, ed. *Command Decisions.* Washington: U.S. Army Center of Military History, 1958.

Greer, Thomas H. *The Development of Air Doctrine in the Army Air Corps, 1917–1941.* Maxwell Air Force Base, Ala.: Air University Press, 1953.

Gruber, Carol S. "Manhattan Project Maverick: The Case of Leo Szilard." *Prologue* 15 (Summer 1983): 73–87.

Hagan, Kenneth J., and William R. Rogers, eds. *Against All Enemies: Interpretations of American Military History from Colonial Times to the Present.* Westport, Conn.: Greenwood Press, 1986.

Halberstam, David. *The Best and the Brightest.* New York: Random House, 1972.

Hallion, Richard P. *Test Pilots: The Frontiersmen of Flight.* Garden City, N.Y.: Doubleday and Company, 1981.

Hansell, Haywood S., Jr. *The Air Plan that Defeated Hitler.* Atlanta: Higgins-McArthur, Longino and Porter, 1972.

——————. *The Strategic Air War Against Germany and Japan: A Memoir.* Washington: Office of Air Force History, 1986.

Hastings, Max. *Bomber Command.* New York: The Dial Press, 1979.

——————. *Overlord: D-Day and the Battle for Normandy.* New York: Simon and Schuster, 1984.

Hayes, Grace P. *The History of the Joint Chiefs of Staff in World War II: The War Against Japan.* Annapolis: Naval Institute Press, 1982.

Hewlett, Richard G., and Oscar E. Anderson, Jr. *The New World, 1939–1946.* [A History of the United States Atomic Energy Commission, Vol. 2]. University Park, Pa.: The Pennsylvannia State University Press, 1962.

Hilsman, Roger. *To Move A Nation.* Garden City, N.Y.: Doubleday and Company, 1967.

Hitch, Charles J. *Decisionmaking for Defense.* Berkeley: University of California Press, 1965.

Hopkins, J. C. "The Development of the Strategic Air Command, 1946–1986." Omaha, Nebr.: Office of the Historian, Headquarters, Strategic Air Command, 1986.

Horelick, Arnold L. "The Cuban Missile Crisis, An Analysis of Soviet Calculations and Behavior." *World Politics* 17 (April 1964): 363–389.

Hurley, Alfred F. *Billy Mitchell: Crusader for Airpower.* Bloomington, Ind.: Indiana University Press, 1964.

Huston, John. "The Wartime Leadership of 'Hap Arnold.'" *Air Power and Warfare, Proceedings of the 8th Military Symposium USAF Academy, October 18–20.* Eds. Alfred F. Hurley and Robert C. Ehrhart. Washington: Office of Air Force History, 1979.

BIBLIOGRAPHY

Iriye, Akira. *Power and Culture: The Japanese American War, 1941–1945.* Cambridge, Mass.: Harvard University Press, 1981.

Kalb, Marvin, and Bernard Kalb. *Kissinger.* Boston: Little, Brown and Company, 1974.

Karnow, Stanley. *Vietnam: A History.* New York: Viking Press, 1983.

Kaufman, William W. *The McNamara Strategy.* New York: Harper and Row, 1964.

Kenney, George C. *General Kenney Reports: A Personal History of the Pacific War.* New York: Duell, Sloan and Pearce, 1949; reprint, Washington: Office of Air Force History, 1987.

Kissinger, Henry. *White House Years.* Boston: Little, Brown and Company, 1979.

Knaack, Marcelle S. *Post-World War II Bombers, 1945–1973.* Washington: Office of Air Force History, 1988.

Kohler, Foy D., and Mose L. Harvey, eds. *The Soviet Union, Yesterday, Today, and Tommorrow.* Coral Gable, Fla.: University of Miami, 1975.

Kohn, Richard H., and Joseph P. Harahan, eds. *Air Interdiction in World War II, Korea, and Vietnam: An Interview with Gen. Earle E. Partridge, Gen. Jacob E. Smart, and Gen. John W. Vogt, Jr.* Washington: Office of Air Force History, 1986.

—————, eds. *Air Superiority in World War II and Korea: An Interview with Gen. James Ferguson, Gen. Robert M. Lee, Gen. William Momyer, and Lt. Gen. Elwood R. Quesada.* Washington: Office of Air Force History, 1983.

—————. "U.S. Strategic Air Power 1948–1962: Excerpts from an Interview with Generals Curtis E. LeMay, Leon W. Johnson, David A. Burchinal, and Jack J. Catton." *International Security* 12 (1988): 78–95.

Korb, Lawrence J. *The Joint Chiefs of Staff: The First Twenty-Five Years.* Bloomington, Ind.: Indiana University Press, 1976.

Kraft, Joseph. *Profiles in Power.* New York: New American Library, 1966.

Layton, Edwin T., *et al. "And I Was There," Pearl Harbor and Midway—Breaking the Secrets.* New York: William Morrow, 1985.

Leffler, Melvyn P. "The American Conception of National Security and the Beginnings of the Cold War, 1945–1948." *American Historical Review* 89 (April 1984): 346–381.

LeMay, Curtis E., and MacKinlay Kantor. *Mission with LeMay: My Story.* New York: Doubleday and Company, 1965.

Levering, Ralph B. *The Cold War, 1945–1987.* 2d ed. Arlington Heights: Ill.: Harlan Davidson, Inc., 1988.

Lewin, Ronald. *The American Magic: Codes, Ciphers, and the Defeat of Japan.* New York: Farrar, Straus, Giroux, 1982.

Lewy, Guenter. *America in Vietnam.* New York: Oxford University Press, 1978.

McCarthy, James R., and George B. Allison. *Linebacker II: A View From the Rock.* Montgomery, Ala.: Air Power Institute, 1979.

MacIsaac, David. *Strategic Bombing in World War II: The Story of the United States Strategic Bombing Survey.* New York: Garland Publishing Company, 1976.

Mastny, Vojtech. *Russia's Road To the Cold War: Diplomacy, Warfare, and the Politics of Communism 1941–1945.* New York: Columbia University Press, 1978.

Medvedev, Roy A., and Zhores A. Medvedev. *Khrushchev: The Years in Power.* New York: Columbia University Press, 1976.

Meisner, Maurice J. *Mao's China: A History of the People's Republic.* New York: Free Press, 1977.

Melosi, Martin M. *The Shadow of Pearl Harbor: Political Controversy Over the Surprise Attack, 1941-1946.* College Station, Tex.: University of Texas Press, 1977.

Miller, Jay. *Lockeed SR-71.* Arlington, Tex.: Aerofax Press, 1985.

Millett, Allan R. *Semper Fidelis: The History of the U.S. Marine Corps.* New York: Macmillan Publishing Company, 1980.

Mitchell, William. *Skyways: A Book of Modern Aeronautics.* New York: J.B. Lippincott, 1930.

—————. *Winged Defense: The Development and Possibilities of Modern Air Power— Economic and Military.* New York: G.P. Putnam's Sons, 1925.

Momyer, William W. *Airpower in Three Wars (WWII, Korea, Vietnam).* Washington: Department of the Air Force, 1978.

Morison, Samuel Elliot. *Victory in the Pacific.* [History of U.S. Naval Operations in World War II, Vol. 14]. Boston: Little, Brown and Company, 1960.

Morrocco, John. *The Vietnam Experience: Thunder From Above, The Air War 1961–1968.* Boston: Boston Publishing Company, 1984.

Munson, Kenneth G. *Aircraft of World War Two.* New York: Doubleday and Company, 1972.

——————. and F. Gordon Swansborough. *Boeing.* New York: Arco Publishing Company, 1972.

Murray, Williamson. *Strategy For Defeat: The Luftwaffe 1933–1945.* Montgomery, Ala.: Air University Press, 1983.

Neustadt, Richard E. *Alliance Politics.* New York: Columbia University Press, 1970.

Newby, Leroy W. *Target Ploesti: View From A Bombsight.* Norvato, Calif.: Presidio Press, 1983.

Newcomb, Richard F. *Iwo Jima.* New York: Holt, Rhinehart, and Winston, 1965.

Nixon, Richard M. *RN, The Memoirs of Richard Nixon.* New York: Grosset and Dunlap, 1978.

Office of Statistical Control. *Army Air Forces Statistical Digest, World War II.* Washington: Headquarters Army Air Forces, 1945.

Overy, R. J. *The Air War 1939–1945.* New York: Stein and Day, 1981.

——————. "The Military and the European Economy 1939–1945." *Militärgeschichtliche Mitteilungen* 21 (February 1979): 55–78.

Paret, Peter, ed. *Makers of Modern Strategy, From Machiavelli to the Nuclear Age.* Princeton, N.J.: Princeton University Press, 1986.

Park, W. Hays. "Linebacker and the Law of War." *Air University Review* 34 (Jan-Feb 1983): 2–30.

Parton, James. *"Air Force Spoken Here": General Ira Eaker and the Command of the Air.* Bethesda, Md.: Adler and Adler, 1986.

Pogue, Forrest C. *General George C. Marshall.* 4 Vols. New York: Viking Press, 1963–1987.

Porter, Gareth. *A Peace Denied: The United States, Vietnam, and the Paris Agreement.* Bloomington, Ind.: Indiana University Press, 1975.

Prang, Gordon. *At Dawn We Slept: The Untold Story of Pearl Harbor.* New York: McGraw-Hill Company, 1981.

Rearden, Steven L. *The Formative Years, 1947–1950.* [History of the Office of the Secretary of Defense, Vol. 1]. Washington: Office of the Secretary of Defense, 1984.

Roberts, Arthur, ed. *Radar Beacons.* New York: McGraw-Hill Company, 1947.

Roherty, James M. *Decisions of Robert S. McNamara: A Study of the Role of the Secretary of Defense.* Coral Gables, Fla.: University of Miami Press, 1970.

Romanus, Charles F., and Riley Sunderland. *Stilwell's Mission To China.* [U.S. Army in World War II: China-Burma-India Theater]. Washington: U.S. Army Center of Military History, 1953.

Rosenberg, David Alan. "American Atomic Stategy and the Hydrogen Bomb Decision." *Journal of American History* 66 (1979): 62–87.

——————. " 'A Smoking Radiating Ruin at the End of Two Hours': Documents on the American Plans for Nuclear War with the Soviet Union." *International Security* 6 (Winter 1981–1982): 3–38.

——————. "U.S. Nuclear Stockpile, 1945 to 1950." *The Bulletin of Atomic Scientists* 38 (May 1982): 25–29.

Rostow, Walt W. *Pre-Invasion Bombing Strategy: General Eisenhower's Decision of March 25, 1944.* Austin, Tex.: University of Texas Press, 1981.

Sagan, Scott D. "Nuclear Alerts and Crisis Management." *International Security* 9 (Spring 1985): 106–122.

Sallager, Frederick M. "Lessons From an Aerial Mining Campaign (Operation 'Starvation')." RAND Report R–1322PR. Santa Monica, Calif.: RAND, April 1974.

Schaffer, Ronald. *Wings of Judgment: American Bombing in World War II.* New York: Oxford University Press, 1985.

BIBLIOGRAPHY

Schlesinger, Arthur M., Jr. *A Thousand Days: John F. Kennedy in the White House.* Boston: Houghton Mifflin, 1965.

Sharp, Ulysses S. Grant. *Strategy For Defeat, Vietnam in Retrospect.* San Rafael, Calif.: Presidio Press, 1978.

Sherry, Michael S. *The Rise of American Air Power: The Creation of Armageddon.* New Haven: Yale University Press, 1987.

Sherwin, Martin J. *A World Destroyed: The Atom Bomb and the Grand Alliance.* New York: Alfred A. Knopf, 1975.

Shiner, John F. *Foulois and the U.S. Army Air Corps, 1931–1935.* Washington: Office of Air Force History, 1983.

Slusser, Robert M. *The Berlin Crisis of 1961.* Baltimore: Johns Hopkins Press, 1973.

Smith, Bruce L. R. *The RAND Corporation.* Cambridge, Mass.: Harvard University Press, 1966.

Spector, Ronald H. *Advice and Support: The Early Years.* [The U.S. Army in Vietnam]. Washington: U.S. Army Center of Military History, 1983.

――――――. *Eagle Against the Sun: The American War with Japan.* New York: Free Press, 1984.

Stokesbury, James L. *A Short History of World War II.* New York: William Morrow and Company, 1980.

Swanborough, F. Gordon, and Peter M. Bowers. *United States Military Aircraft Since 1909.* New York: Putnam, 1963.

Swenson, Loyd S. Jr., James M. Grimwood, and Charles C. Alexander. *This New Ocean: A History of Project Mercury.* Washington: National Aeronautics and Space Administration, 1966.

Taylor, John W.R., ed. *Jane's All The World's Aircraft, 1969–1970.* London: Jane's Publishing Company, 1970.

Taylor, Maxwell D. *The Uncertain Trumpet.* New York: Harper and Row, 1960.

Terraine, John. *A Time For Courage: The Royal Air Force in the European War, 1939–1945.* New York: MacMillan Publishing Company, 1985.

Thompson, James C. *Rolling Thunder, Understanding Policy and Program Failure.* Chapel Hill, N.C.: University of North Carolina Press, 1980.

Thompson, Wayne, ed. *Air Leadership.* Washington: Office of Air Force History, 1986.

Thorne, Christopher. *Allies of A Kind: The United States, Britain, and the War Against Japan.* New York: Oxford University Press, 1978.

Trachtenberg, Marc. "The Influence of Nuclear Weapons in the Cuban Missile Crisis." *International Security* 10 (Summer 1985): 137-163.

――――――. "White House Tapes and the Minutes of the Cuban Missile Crisis." *International Security* 10 (Summer 1985): 164–203.

Trewhitt, Henry L. *McNamara.* New York: Harper and Row, 1971.

Truman, Harry S. *Memoirs of Harry S Truman: Years of Decision.* New York: Doubleday and Company, 1955.

Tuchman, Barbara W. *Stilwell and the American Experience in China, 1911-45.* New York: MacMillan, 1971.

Tunner, William H. *Over the Hump.* New York: Duell, Sloan and Pearce, 1964; reprint, Washington: Office of Air Force History, 1985.

United States Strategic Bombing Survey, Europe. 208 Reports. Washington: Government Printing Office, 1945.

United States Strategic Bombing Survey, Pacific. 108 Reports. Washington: Government Printing Office, 1946.

United States Congress. House. Committee on Foreign Affairs. *The War Powers Resolution* by John H. Sullivan. Committee print. Washington: Government Printing Office, 1982.

United States Department of Defense. *The Pentagon Papers: The Senator Gravel Edition,* 4 vols. Boston: Beacon Press, 1971.

Verrier, Anthony. *The Bombing Offensive.* London: Macmillan Publishing Company, 1968.

Waters, Andrew W. *All the U.S. Air Force Airplanes 1907–1983.* New York: Hippocrene Books, 1983.

Webster, Charles K., and Noble Frankland. *The Strategic Air Offensive Against Germany 1939–1945.* [History of the Second World War]. 4 Vols. London: Her Majesty's Printing Office, 1961–1965.

Weigley, Russell F. *The American Way of War: A History of United States Military Strategy and Policy.* Bloomington, Ind.: Indiana University Press, 1973.

Werrell, Kenneth P. "The Strategic Bombing of Germany in World War II: Costs and Accomplishments." *Journal of American History* 73 (December 1986): 702–713.

Welch, David A., and James F. Blight. "The Eleventh Hour of the Cuban Missile Crisis: An Introduction to the Excomm Transcripts." *International Security* 12 (1987/88): 5–29.

Westmoreland, William C. *A Soldier Reports.* Garden City, N.Y.: Doubleday and Company, 1976.

Wohlstetter, Roberta. *Pearl Harbor: Warning and Decision.* Stanford, Calif.: Stanford University Press, 1962.

Wolff, Leon. *Low Level Mission.* New York: Doubleday and Company, 1957.

Wolk, Herman S. *Planning and Organizing the Postwar Air Force 1943–1947.* Washington: Office of Air Force History, 1982.

Yergin, Daniel. *Shattered Peace: Origins of the Cold War and the National Security State.* Boston: Houghton Mifflin, 1977.

Zuckerman, Solly. *From Apes to Warlords: The Autobiography (1904–1946) of Solly Zuckerman.* New York: Harper and Row, 1978.

Index

Ahmann, Hugh N.: 2
Air Corps: 21, 21n. 5
Air Corps Tactical School. *See* Army Air
    Corps Tactical School
Air Divisions
    Third: 10
    817th: 16
    821st: 16
    822d: 16
Air Force
    formative concepts: 2
    overall purpose: 111–12
    post-World War II: 82
    wartime capability: 108–09
Air Force Council: 13
"Air Force Day" raid on Japan: 70
Air Force Logistics Command: 11, 17 (earlier,
    Air Technical Service Command)
Air Forces (numbered)
    Seventh: 127n.148
    Eighth: 4, 8, 23n, 27n, 30n.18, 31n.19, 32n,
        33n.23, 36n, 41n.31, 42n, 43n.34, 47n
    Ninth: 37n.27, 45n.36
    Tenth: 37n.27
    Fifteenth: 10, 16, 37n.27, 68, 73, 81
    Twentieth (formerly, XXI Bomber Com-
        mand): 30n.18, 48n.39, 53n.46, 61, 90
Air interdiction: 1, 47, 87
Air power: 2, 21, 22n, 28 *See also* Strategic
    Operations
Air refueling: 104–05, 105n.116
Air Task Groups: 15 *See also* CROSSROADS
Air Technical Service Command. *See* Air
    Force Logistics Command
Aircraft types, Germany
    FW 190: 32n
    Me–109: 45
    Me–209a: 44
    Me–262 (jet): 44
Aircraft types, Great Britain
    Vulcan: 110n.126
    Wellington: 26
Aircraft types, United States. *See also*
    Bomber aircraft

A–20: 31
B–1/Keystone: 20
B–2/Curtiss Condor: 20
B–10 (Martin): 20
B–17: 3, 4, 14, 23n, 24–27, 31n.19, 32n, 34,
    42, 71
B–18: 31
B–24: 8, 23, 24n.10, 31n, 41n.31, 45n.36
B–29: 6, 12, 13, 24n.10, 31n.20, 39, 40n,
    48n.39, 51–60, 87, 96
B–36: 6, 13, 24, 108
B–47: 7, 13, 106, 108
B–50: 13, 92
B–50A: 7, 104n
B–52: 7, 13, 107–08, 126
B–58: 7
DC–3: 31n.20
DH–4 (de Havilland): 19, 20n.2
DH–4M (modified type): 19n
KB–29: 104
KC–97: 107
KC–135: 106–07
P–35: 20, 21n.4
P–38: 32n
P–47: 21n.4, 24n.10
P–51: 24n.10
SR–71: 110
U–2: 115–17
Anderson, Frederick L: 43, 43n.33
Anderson, Orvil A.: 13, 36n, 82–83, 83n.86
Anderson, Jr., Rudolph: 115n.131
ARC LIGHT: 127
Armstrong, Frank A.: 33n.23
Army Air Corps Tactical School: 8, 29, 32,
    28n.15
Arnold, Henry H.: 5, 31n.19, 48n.39, 52, 68
    biography: 63n.58
    commanding general, Army Air Forces and
        commander, Twentieth Air Force: 52n.45
    and General Marshall: 63
    on German surrender: 69
Artillery: 33n.24
Atlas missile: 100n.110, 102n.113

141

143